Library and Archives Canada Cataloguing in Publication

Lockhart, Art
Restorative justice: transforming society
Art Lockhart and Lynn Zammit

Includes bibliographical references.

ISBN 1-895418-58-5

1. Restorative Justice.   I.Lockhart, Art II. Title

HV8688.Z35 2005   364.6'8   C2005-901061-4

First Edition - 2005

Printing: Copywell, Toronto, Canada. 2019

Inclusion Press
24 Thome Crescent • Toronto • Ontario • M6H 2S5 • Canada
Tel: 416-658-5363   Fax: 416-658-5067
inclusionpress@inclusion.com
www.inclusion.com

D1402364

Note to Readers

This book is designed to be used in conjunction with a three day training workshop that is provided by Art Lockhart and Lynn Zammit. For more information, contact:

Art Lockhart (416) 675-6622, ext. 3354, or e-mail: ***alockhart@sympatico.ca***
Lynn Zammit: e-mail: ***lynn.zammit@sympatico.ca***

Acknowledgements:

The people who are willing to be adventurous enough to explore new ways of seeing, acting and being in the evolving world of social justice. People who have influenced the creation of this book are Rupert Ross, Ruth Morris, David Moore, Art Biffis, Angel Yung, Gerry McClelland, Richard Waugh, Donna Brady, Sam Chaiton, Terry Swinton, Anne Schnider, Oolagen Community Services, Hinks Dellcrest, Rittenhouse, Turning Point, Downsview Conflict Mediation Services, First Charge Program of Owen Sound, the George Hall Centre, the Griffin Centre, Toronto Catholic and District School Boards, Toronto Police Services, and to all the members of the Restorative Justice Network who have helped to keep the dream alive.

Table of Contents

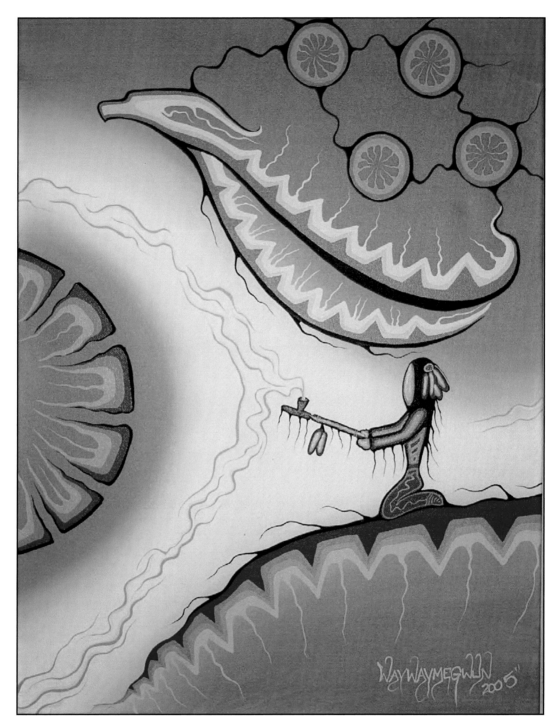

 # 46
"Flowing Energy"

With sacred pipe in hand, we pray with words and thoughts of a life that dances gentle in harmony with the energy of all things. When we try to go force our way through obstacles we sometimes fall and have to start the journey again. But when we take the time to view these obstacles--anger, frustration, desperation—as energy to be embraced, we can learn to flow around any obstacle, living a life of gentleness and peace.

If Walls Could Talk

Randall Charboneau
Waywaymegwun – Swaying Feather

With tear gas burning my eyes, the screaming sound of silence echoed off the cold steel walls. Just another murder, just another lock down, just another day. The irony is that there is no safety or security for the inmates in a violent maximum security institution if one is wanted dead. I was prisoner 596482B serving a sentence of seventeen years for robberies with violence, aggravated assault, and weapons.

Another morning upon me and plenty of time to pass, I said to myself why not try to draw something. I was tired of reading and watching the same old scenes filling the television screen. I remembered I had an old piece of Bristol board, stained with coffee, behind my desk. I pulled it out. I dusted off the tear gas that settled on my desk. With every move I made, the tear gas would rise to burn my eyes once again. As I sat there, wondering what to draw, I looked down at my tattooed arms. The images of skulls excited me, then. That was where I was at in my everyday thinking. I was a young man filled with anger and hatred. No one could comprehend what I felt. I hated the world. I hated myself. With pencil in hand, I slowly traced through the outline of a skull. Then as I continued to draw, I added whatever looked cool, whatever looked violent.

Outside my door, the Goon Squad appears, dressed like aliens in black bullet proof vests, hard helmets and goggles, shields, tear gas canisters at the ready. The door slides open six inches and a small brown lunch bag lands on the floor beside the toilet. Inside the bag is a squished bologna sandwich signed with the footprint of a guard's boot, a badly bruised apple, and a warm, passed-date, small carton of sour milk. My meal for the rest of the day is served.

The final touch to my drawing was a border of barbed wire surrounding a bunch of skulls and bones. It was an image of a cemetery. It was my vision of what this prison looked like from within. Death surrounded me every moment. If only these walls could talk.

After weeks of being locked down, we were finally released to pursue our everyday life events in this world within a world. I had shown my friends what I had drawn and guys would say, "Wow man! Why don't you do that on glass? That would look great!"

I thought about it and decided to go down to the purchasing clerk to order materials. I ordered six pieces of glass, frames, and special ink pens. My journey into the art world had begun. I traced, drew from memory, and created images that seemed to bring orders from people all around me. I become known as a great glass painter in this small prison world. I was proud; I had found something that passed my time. It supplied me with extra money to buy materials, increase my canteen spending, and buy my small pieces of hashish or a joint.

Time passed between numerous lock downs, murders, suicides, mini riots, and demonstrations. The anger within me grew. I became the cold steel walls that surrounded me. I lost hope. Who cares???!!!!

One day I returned to my cell from being out in the yard to discover my cell turned upside down. Photos of my family had been ripped in half. The guards had obviously searched my cell while I was outside. I was enraged!!!

I walked down to the tower and yelled at the guard who sat in there. "You bastards! There's no need for that! "

"Someone's going to pay for this!" I said to myself.

The next morning, the anger burning within me, I walked through the hallways on the way to my job within the prison. Someone was going to pay for destroying my cell. The Warden happened to be standing in the centre of the prison area, surrounded by eight guards watching the prisoners' movement early Monday morning. I knew this Warden and he knew me. I was once on the committee that represented the prisoners. I recalled what he said to me one day. "If you ever have a problem, then tell me and hopefully we can work it out." He was referring to problems with the general population, not individual problems. I walked through the metal detector and stormed between two guards standing in front of the Warden. "Good morning, Mr. Charboneau."

It's not a good morning! One of your goons went in my cell and ripped it apart on the weekend.

"Well, this is a maximum security institution."

Instantly I felt insulted. First of all, I knew exactly where I was, and secondly, he had said it loudly in front of his guards to show his authority by belittling me.

"Is that right?" I pushed him away allowing me to get the space to punch him. The first punch landed on his nose, breaking it.   He started to go down and with an upper cut I snapped his head upwards. Then there were hands and bodies grabbing, smothering me.   I was pulled up by my hair and pushed against the wall. A set of handcuffs snapped my wrists together behind my back. Quickly I was escorted down to the segregation area, the Hole.

The lead guard looked at me. "Charboneau! We have no problem with you, do you have a problem with us?" As they surrounded me.

"No, I got who I wanted" I said.

"We are going to take the cuffs off. If you get undressed so we can search you for weapons and then go directly into the cell, there will be no problems." The guard said. "OK." And away I went.

I was charged for aggravated assault and received an extra five months. Then I was placed in the Special Handling Unit (the SHU) in Quebec.

When you go to the SHU there is a label that attaches to you. I was now considered one of Canada's most dangerous offenders. I was surrounded with Canada's most dangerous men. "Killers." Some killed one man, some killed many men.   Mostly they bragged about how they enjoyed the look on their victims' faces. They were to never see the outside of a prison. To bring excitement to their everyday state of boredom and hopelessness, they plotted to kill other inmates and rationalized their deeds.

I lived with these men and everyday we would spend hours together in a very small cement yard, training, boxing, running, and doing push ups. I knew I would have to get to their level of thinking in order to avoid becoming one of their victims. One day I confronted the boss of one of the crews, a dangerous man and a violent killer. He could clearly see the seriousness of my anger. "You're a crazy guy," he laughed, "there's no problem." That day I gained much respect from the rest of the guys.

I don't remember the day, but I was walking back and forth passing the time. Suddenly, I stopped in the middle of the yard. It was like an aura had come over me. I looked up to the sky, then looked down and stared at the barbed wire fence. I said to myself, "Is this what you want with your life?"

"No!" I said to myself.

From that moment on my life took a drastic turn. I returned to my cell and as I sat on my bed, I flipped through a book in which I had written many poems. As I read them, I shook my head in disbelief seeing, for the first time, where my head and thoughts were at. In every poem, images of killing, death, and hatred. I ripped up that book and proceeded to go through my cell and get rid of any negative material. In the following months, I ordered books on Native culture. I wanted to read about my Ancestors. I wanted to know what had happened to our people. I had to keep in mind that what I was reading was written by non-natives, and most of the accounts were probably very false. But yet I wanted to read about my Ancestors. One book stayed with me: **Returning to the Teachings** by Rupert Ross. The child on the cover of the book has no face, but I could see my face in that painting. Many years later, I would sit with Rupert and share this story with him,. Never in my wildest dreams would I have thought that sitting, talking and sharing with Rupert would be possible.

I was returned to a maximum security institution. I started going to Native Brotherhood meetings and Ceremonies--Sweat Lodge Ceremonies, Pipe Circles, and sitting many hours with the visiting Elders talking about our lives and Traditional Teachings.

I was sitting in a common room with a Native Brother, my best friend, watching him paint. He was an excellent artist and painted only Native themes that were spiritually based. My friend said to me that he had some extra paint and a few pieces of wood. I started drawing images of things I had felt while in the sweat lodge. My friend saw some of my images and encouraged me to paint them.

He showed me how to make my own canvas. We took my bed sheet and cut it in half. For many months, I never had sheets to sleep on. Then we retrieved a few pieces of wood and made a stretcher. After I soaked the bed sheet, I stretched it across the wood frame and stapled it. While it was still wet, I applied a coat of white latex paint and allowed it to dry. When that was dry, I added another coat which would become my primed canvas. I didn't have a paint brush, but quickly realized that I could make my own, cutting a piece of my long hair with a broken shaving razor and then taping it to a pencil.

My first painting was with a brush made of my hair on a canvas made from the sheet on which I slept. The paint was stolen from the paint shop.

The initial images to appear on my canvas excited me. These images were of common animals, mostly the Eagle and the Bear. Many of images to come were ceremonial. No skulls, no violence.

As time passed I was again transferred to a lower security setting where I had a lot more movement around the institution. I became involved in The Native Brotherhood and was recognized as the Spiritual Coordinator. My job was to coordinate Sweat Lodge Ceremonies, Visiting Elders and Helpers, Healing Circles, and Drumming Sessions. As my strength grew spiritually, my artwork became vibrant, colorful, and pure. Everyone wanted my work.

One day, the Ministry Chaplin, Sister Marilyn, asked if she could talk to me. She had heard about me from another Minister who happened to be part Native. Sister Marilyn invited me into her office and asked me if I was interested in reading a book. I thought it was going to be **God's Prison Gang** in which I had no interest. To my surprise it was called **Healing the Child Within**. For the next year I read this book and did the exercises in it. As each night passed, I cried into my pillow like a child, releasing all the pain, guilt, and shame built up within me.

The journey of healing has many paths and many doorways. A year before I was released, I met a few wonderful women at Native Brotherhood Socials, all of whom were willing to help me when I got out. The time was near for me to be released on mandatory supervision. Sixteen years of prison life under my belt, one year on parole left.

Within two weeks of being released, I had an interview with the Executive Director of an Art Gallery, thanks to those women who had promised to help me. Carol Hill, the Director, knew of my situation and said she was willing to give me a chance. For the next two years I was the gallery coordinator. I was involved in everything. My personal life in the art scene had taken a turn for the better. It seemed that I had learned so much in so little time. Life was for the first time truly becoming real.

In three years, I had accomplished so much. I received an Emerging Artist Grant from the Ontario Arts Council; I exhibited in over twenty group and Solo Exhibitions. I was doing artist talks; I painted a wall mural inside a youth prison. The newspapers stared calling, wanting to do articles on me. The first was the *Hamilton Spectator,* the largest was the *Toronto Star.* They did a page and a half feature on me for Canada Day (2004). A video documentary was started. I made presentations to Police Foundation students at community colleges.

My life is changing again as I focus on working to heal the at-risk youth through story-telling and art. I was invited to tell my story to the youth at the Strict Discipline School in Brampton. These kids have been expelled from regular school due to criminal activity. They range in age from thirteen to eighteen. I continue talk with them regularly. Some visits are individual sessions with the kids who want to share their private stories. At other times I work with a group. I make presentations on my life and my art. I explain what the images represent to me, and my healing journey through life. I teach about the Native experience through Native images. This presentation leads to painting workshops where the kids talk about their images. I have gained their trust and I encourage them to express themselves through the arts and the images they create.

Just as the image on Rupert's book represents for me the child returning to the teachings, I too am continuing to return to the teachings. And one of the main themes of my talks is about peeling away the layers and masks to find the child within. I was a child that did not know love, a child that was abused, a child that knew neglect by the adults I trusted. And as I move upward in my journey, I realize that sharing voice is important. It is vital to everyone's healing experience. Along this way, one voice that needs to be heard is the voice of the person who has been victimized by the forms of behaviour I personified. I feel for the people I have harmed, and I want so much to tell those I have harmed that I am truly sorry. I need them to know that I want to hear their voice, hear their story. For when we can hear, truly hear one another's voice, the healing, restoration and transformation can honestly begin, for all of us. We all have our stories, be they sad or beautiful. They make us who we are.

If these walls could talk, they would tell the story of healing.

#50
"CHI-MEEGWETCH MIGIZI—BIG THANK YOU--"

It is that spirit of the eagle which we honour. For there was a time when the earth was going to be destroyed by the Creator's Helper because of the never-ending wars and conflicts people had created. But between the darkness of night and the lightness of dawn the eagle flew through and called out 4 times gaining the Creator's attention. The Creator stopped his Helper from destroying the earth. The eagle said to the Creator—there are still some people who are living good lives and that future generations of their children would continue in good ways. The eagle asked the Creator to honour these people and help them to discover ways to end the wars and conflicts. The Creator agreed to the eagle's request, and today we say Thank You to that eagle.

Exploring Criminal Justice
and
The Aboriginal Healing Paradigm

Rupert Ross
Assistant Crown Attorney
Ontario Ministry of the Attorney General

All of the opinions expressed herein are personal to the author,
and do not in any fashion reflect the perspectives or policies of the Government of Ontario.

A. Introduction

I remember a Cree grandmother from Saskatchewan passing some of her teachings to a group of aboriginal youngsters. At one point she startled everyone by slapping her thigh and exclaiming "You know, I think I finally figured out what it means to live *a good life*".

"Maybe, " she told us, "You know you're living a good life when you get to my age, and you look back maybe five years or so, and you find yourself saying 'Boy, I sure didn't know too much… way back then!".

I enjoy the picture she gave me that day, the sense that I will always be given deeper questions as I stumble through my allotted years. But her teaching suggested something else as well: if I acknowledge that every five years or so I'll probably change my advice to **myself**, why would I try to give anyone else advice along the way?

Instead, all I can do is tell my stories as best I can. If others happen to find them useful in some way, within *their* unique experience of life, well, that's a bonus.

And that's the spirit in which I'll try to write, as a co-explorer who is not quite sure where he'll end up next!

I have been a criminal prosecutor for 19 years, working primarily in remote aboriginal communities in northwestern Ontario. Sadly, some communities experience such high levels of family violence and sexual abuse that, if we ever achieved full disclosure and full victim/witness cooperation in court, we'd be jailing well over 50% of the adult population. No one sees that result as constructive; in fact, many **victims** choose not to bring their problems into our adversarial and punitive system because they don't want that result.

Instead, we hear an insistent call for something called "**healing** justice". I was given a chance to explore that phrase during a three-year posting with the federal Department of Justice, travelling from the Atlantic to the Pacific.

At the very start of my exploration, a Mi'kmaw grandmother in Nova Scotia encouraged me not to just investigate specific healing programs but to spend equal time with the Elders, the teachers and the philosophers. She was concerned that I might never come to understand the programs I encountered unless I first gained some understanding of how aboriginal people understood Creation in general, and the proper place of mankind within it. I will be forever grateful for her guidance, for I have since learned that the aboriginal preference for healing is not just a preference at all, but a necessary manifestation of a world-view that is fundamentally at odds with the Cartesian, Newtonian and Darwinian world-view in which I grew up.

In the course of my travels, I came across many different programs in aboriginal communities. One community had already spent a decade putting traditional understandings to work in an effective and sophisticated response to sexual abuse, using powerful, healing-centered interventions in the lives of offenders, victims, relatives, friends and the community at large. It is not my intention to provide details about that specific program, but to speak more generally about what I now think of as a different healing **paradigm** at work with many aboriginal people, whether on this continent or in other parts of the aboriginal globe, and whether the crime being addressed is sexual abuse, family violence - or children breaking windows.

Paradigms are hard to talk about, however, because you have to substantially escape your own to even **hear** what is being said about another. For that reason, I'm going to begin by describing the tiniest portion of the cross-cultural Magical Mystery Tour which, thanks to that Mi'kmaw grandmother, became my life for those three years.

B.   Gaining the Relational Lens

My time immersed in aboriginal teachings has given me something I think of as a "relational lens". When I look through it, it changes how I see almost everything. I cannot take you through **all** the struggles involved in gaining it, but mentioning a few may give some sense of what I mean.

I remember, for instance, being told that western and aboriginal scientists might approach the study of a plant in very different ways. The western scientist might focus most of her attention on understanding and naming all the parts and properties of the plant, figuring out its root, stem and leaf patterns, how it takes in water, sunlight and nutrients, how it reproduces, its life expectancy, and so forth. The aboriginal scientist, by contrast, would likely focus most of her attention on understanding what role that plant plays in the meadow. She would examine how it holds soil when the rains come, what plants flourish close to it, what birds, animals and insects are attracted to it, how it is useful to them, what kinds of conditions it needs to remain healthy, that sort of thing. It's not that the two scientists pay **no** attention to the concerns of the other, just that their emphasis is different. They 'see' the plant in different ways.

I had no idea how a teaching like that might relate to justice, but I couldn't shake the Mi'kmaw grandmother's encouragement to keep my horizons wide and open. I built a special shelf in my memory, labeled it 'Indian Puzzles', and stuffed that plant-in-the-meadow story up there, hoping that one day I might figure out the connection.

Everywhere I went it was the same!

I was told that western and aboriginal cultures hold opposite views about the importance of human beings in Creation. The Bible puts us right at the top, set on earth to rule all the fishes in the sea, everything. Aboriginal teachings seem to present an opposite hierarchy. Mother Earth (with her life-blood, the waters) plays the most important role in Creation, for without the soil and water there would be no plant realm. Without the plants there would be no animal realm, and without soil, water, plants and animals, there would be no us. Within this 'reverse hierarchy', human creatures are understood to be the least essential and the most dependant; no longer masters of Creation, we are its humble servants.

It was not how I was used to seeing myself!

After speaking of things like that, aboriginal teachers would often turn to me and ask "How can we accept your justice system when our world-view is so completely different?" And I would silently scream "Wait! I haven't the faintest idea why seeing Creation in a way that puts broccoli on a higher plane than your best buddies would lead to different visions of justice!". But I'd keep quiet, put that reverse-hierarchy on my Indian Puzzles Shelf, and carry on.

It got worse. I remember an Elder saying: "Your people seem to think that law comes from books. That's not the way my people understand it." He turned towards a window, pointed out to dense bush and announced "THAT'S where law comes from!". All I could think of was "Whoa! I know what kind of law is out there. Darwin told me: it's The Law of the Jungle! Where we live in dog-eat-dog anarchy, acting like ANIMALS towards each other! Isn't that exactly what man-made law is designed to control?". I didn't say that, of course, because I'd often heard him giving his teachings, and he always spoke of values like respect, love, caring, sharing and humility. How did he get those values from the bush? Which one of us was missing something? Why did I think it was me?

One more. At the opening of an aboriginal justice conference in the mountains of Alberta, a large shell was brought around, filled with smoldering sweetgrass. Each of us wafted that beautifully-scented smoke over our heads, eyes, ears, mouths, chests and thighs, asking for its assistance to think, see, hear, speak and feel only in healthy and respectful ways during our time together. The discussion leader, a Blackfoot lawyer and professor, then spoke about language differences, explaining that aboriginal languages were not as much noun-centered as they were verb-centered, trying to emphasize not the thing-aspect of Creation but the pattern, flow and function aspect. He held that shell in his hands and told us that in aboriginal languages it would be 'called' differently at different times. It could be a sacred vessel at one calling, a vessel bringing candy at another, or a vessel receiving cigarette butts at another; it depended on its relationship to the speaker and to the occasion. To call it, as European languages did, by one name for all occasions was seen as a 'poorer' way to speak of the world. Indian eyes, he told us, when they look upon Creation, see a much more fluid, transforming and interconnecting reality than Newton ever did, with his linear, billiard-ball chains of cause and effect.

While the discussion was fascinating, I still had to wonder: why I was being told these things at a **justice** conference?

Then, one beautiful August day, a very small event hit me in a very large way. I encountered an Ojibway grandmother hitch-hiking in northwestern Ontario and I gave her a lift. Knowing that a lot of the old people gather blueberries to raise a little cash, I asked her how the blueberry crop was that summer. She immediately replied "Oh, I was at the garbage dump last night, and there were SIXTEEN BEARS out there!". I had lived in the north long enough to understand her answer: bears thrive on blueberries, and a failed blueberry crop causes hungry bears to converge on the nearest dumps in search of food. Conversely, a bumper crop means all the bears are back in the blueberry patches sporting huge purple grins!

But it was the automatic way she answered that got to me. I could feel all the teachings I had jammed onto my Indian Puzzles Shelf doing little two-steps around each other, like they were finally organizing around a theme. I had asked about one **thing**, but had received an answer that referred to a totally **separate thing** instead. It started coming: things weren't separate to her at all, not the way they were to me. Instead, all things acted within complex webs of **relationships**. Whatever happened with one thing rippled out to touch and affect all other things. If you talked about one, you were talking about all. And any point of reference would do.

It moved a little further. To her, the real essence of Creation lay in what was going on **between** things. That's where her attention went, to all the relationships that bind things together so strongly that a question about blueberries gets an answer about bears!

As I chewed that over, connections with the teachings I'd been given started revealing themselves. The plant-in-the-meadow teaching, for instance, where the well-educated aboriginal eye sees not the plant in isolation but the vast web of relationships connecting it with all the other things that make up the meadow: if you look at it that way, the meadow is, *in its essence*, less a collection of things than a complex of ever-modifying relationships.

If, that is, the eye learns to focus between, rather than on.

Relationships. I started kicking myself: didn't every sweat lodge end with everyone exclaiming "All My Relations", where relations included the earth, the sky, everything? How long had I known that, but never seen how central it was?

I began to see where the 'reverse hierarchy' of Creation came from. If your way-of-knowing focuses on relationships, it will be 'natural' to see that the relationships between human, animal, plant and earth/water aspects of Creation are fundamentally relationships of **dependency,** with us at the bottom, as the most dependent. If, however, your way-of-knowing focuses instead on separate things and their properties, human creatures will 'naturally' stand out as near the top, given our unique powers of communication, movement, tool-making and the like. And from that lofty vantage point it would only be 'natural' to put the deaf, dumb, stupid and immobile plant world right down at the bottom of the heap.

Relationships. The naming of the shell showed the same emphasis: it was the relationship between it, the person using it and the occasion of its use which shaped the way it would be called at any point in time. Change any part of the dynamic and the naming changes with it.

Looking between, amongst and around, not at.

When the Elder had pointed out the window to the bush as the source of law, it was not **things** he directed me towards, but **relationships**. What he saw, what his teachings helped him see, was a totality defined primarily by healthy, sustaining, *symbiotic* relationships between all the things out there. While bears need fish need frogs need insects need algae need water needs sunlight and so forth, they are not so much **linear** chains of dependency as they are interwoven mutualities of such complexity that no one can truly 'know' what will happen if one element changes its contribution to - its relationship with - the mix. All we can say is that they are all **necessary** to each other, to us, and to the relationships which sustain us. In the language of the Elders, they are all sacred.

And the fundamental law to be discerned from aboriginal observation of the symbiotic dynamism of the natural order is not Darwin's entity-centered law of violent competition, but the Law of Respect. Each entity makes essential and unique contributions to the maintenance of a healthy whole. And every contribution, whether positive or negative, touches all. Within this vision, matter is little more than the medium through which patterned **forces** manifest themselves, and it is those patterned forces, not the matter they push around, which are the true essence of Creation. Aboriginal teachings suggest we direct the bulk of our attention towards those patterning forces if we wish to maintain ourselves - and our universe - in health.

Over time, as the teachings on my Indian Puzzles began to reveal the coherence of their underlying vision, the 'relational lens' began to take on increasing force, causing me to wonder what the world would look like if I learned to use it every day. Little did I suspect how substantial the changes would be!

C. Re-defining 'The Crime'

I recall a case where a young offender went into the home of a middle-aged couple while they were away, slipping through an unlocked patio door to steal a bottle of rum. In the offender's eyes, all he did was steal a bottle. As the court saw it, while he had indeed invaded their privacy, it was 'only' for a quick moment, involved no physical confrontation, and only resulted in a $20 loss.

In speaking with the victims, however, it became clear that it was not just a minor property crime to them. Every noise in the night now caused them to bolt upright in bed. Their home was no longer a place of comfort and security, but a vulnerable place, open to threat.

When I applied the relational lens, I found a different way to articulate what had taken place: that crime had significantly injured their **relationship with their home**. Being relational in nature, that injury remained long after the property-centered case was declared 'closed'.

Questions began to emerge. When victims complain that the court has never really 'heard' them, is it because neither the court nor the offender have ever defined the crime in the same way that victims **experience** it, as causing an enduring injury to central relationships in their lives? Are victims even **able** to articulate their injury in that way, or has our 'thing-centered' way of looking at the world kept us from recognizing that what is truly injured by crime is our capacity for maintaining or creating healthy relationships?

Another case. A woman was walking down the street in her town when an angry, muttering stranger suddenly veered towards her, grabbed her purse and ran. She was not hurt, but she no longer felt safe on the streets of her own community. She worried that every man coming her way might turn out to be another attacker. Under the relational lens, the real crime was against her **relationship with the streets of her neighborhood**. Seen in that way, it was not just a ten-second, once-only event, but something which would continue to infect her way-of-relating to her community long into the future. It is likely that the offender believed he had 'only' stolen a purse, and the court characterized it as a 'momentary threat' and a 'minor' property loss. It may even be that the victim, at the conscious level, shared that characterization, wondering what was wrong with **her** that her life seemed so dramatically changed by such a 'small' event.

But it is was sexual assault cases which really showed me the validity of the relational lens. I recall two women describing how their rapes many years earlier had changed everything in their lives. One said she still felt so dirty that, whenever her grandchildren crawled up on her lap, she had to shoo them away. Those children had no idea why their grandmother 'didn't want them', and she couldn't tell them. The real crime was against her capacity to engage in warm and embracing **relationships with other human beings**, even her own grandchildren. The other woman said that, after 14 years, the sight of her own body still repels her so strongly that whenever she goes into someone's bathroom, she opens the medicine cabinet and turns the mirror to the wall so she can't see her own reflection. Her rape had twisted and poisoned her **relationship with her own body**. "Maybe", she wondered aloud, "that's why I stay so fat, take such poor care of my body, because I can't stand living in it."

I also remember the words of a man who had been sexually abused as a child many years earlier: "For me, it's finished 24 years now, and it still haunts me, every day. This morning when I woke up, my wife there kissed me and says 'You know, I love you.' I just turned around and said 'I don't know what love is', because I don't trust no one." His capacity for warm, reciprocal and trusting relationships had been extensively damaged, carrying the impact of that crime far into the future, affecting the lives of all who dealt with him, especially those who wanted to love him the most.

Those kinds of experiences have caused me to start **defining** crimes differently, as events which have immediate and enduring impacts on every victim's ability to maintain - or develop - healthy relationships, whether with their towns, their neighborhoods, their homes, their friends, their loved ones, their bodies, their sense-of-self, or any combination of those essential aspects of a healthy life.

An Inuit grandmother expressed this perspective very succinctly during a sentencing where the offender had sexually touched her granddaughter while he was a visitor in their small Nunavuut community, once in the church while she was playing piano, and once in the school while she was working on a shop project. What she told the sentencing court in Kenora (via video link-up with Nunavuut) was this:

"We have to help her try and rebuild the trust that he destroyed: the trust that she had in the church, the trust that she had in the school system, and the trust that she had with adults"

Interestingly, she also spoke about how sorry she now was for the offender. Her community had seen that he had been given a very special gift, the ability to relate well with children, and they had valued his help in counseling suicidal youngsters. However, he had "abused his gift" by what he had done, and now the court was going to forbid him from being able to use it in the future, because he would not be allowed to be alone with children. That, she told us, was what happens when you don't respect the gifts you are given.

Once I began to wear the relational lens more frequently, and to think of crimes as primarily **relational** events, I found myself reviewing some of the fundamental tenets of the criminal justice system - and discovering that they weren't nearly as sophisticated as I had always thought!

D. 'Justice' within the Relational Paradigm

For one thing, our system shows an almost fanatical determination to focus on acts alone. It is particular acts that must be carefully alleged, then proven in court 'beyond a reasonable doubt'. Those same acts then largely determine the court's response, because we believe that 'the punishment must fit the crime'. I recall doing a full-day trial where there was no disagreement about who injured whom, why, and exactly what the injury was. The only issue was whether the injury was serious enough to convict him for 'assault causing bodily harm', or just for plain assault. The choice of label would then tell us what kind of sentence we'd impose - even though it added not a single piece of information!

In aboriginal approaches, the act is seen primarily as a signal of disharmonies within the offender's relational life, disharmonies which must be addressed if there is any hope of preventing further criminal behavior. Once the act is understood, the spotlight shines elsewhere.

The criminal justice system also seems to believe that it can deal effectively with offenders strictly as **individuals,** for they stand alone in the prisoner's box, whether at trial or at sentencing. It also seems to believe that individuals can simply **choose** to alter their behavior. We threaten people with punishment in the belief that our threats will force them to make better choices. We regularly ship troubled youngsters off to treatment facilities, for instance, hoping that a few more skills will enable them to make better choices. When they go right back to making poor choices within days of returning home, we scratch our heads and wonder: did they just get *poor* treatment, or not *enough* treatment – or is this just a truly *bad* kid?

The relational analysis, by contrast, begins with the proposition that the tide of dysfunctional relations swirling around individuals is, in many cases, simply too powerful to resist, no matter how skilled and determined an individual person (especially a youngster!) might be. If progress is to be made, then all of those relationships must be brought into the process so that everyone can see the need to make better choices, and be given help in making them **together.** To reach back to the Indian Puzzles Shelf, if a plant in the meadow is ill, then the eye must to turn to all of the relationships which sustained it before and which are less than sustaining now.

It was a Cree grandmother from northern Quebec who really showed me the power of this relational lens. We were talking about family violence, and she was concerned about our insistence on taking abusive men out to jail. "We know you do this to protect the women and children," she told me, "but to protect us in your way, you would have to keep them there forever. Since you don't, we'd like to try our way instead." When I asked what her way was, she said something along the following lines: "In our understanding, anyone who can act in these ways towards others has somehow learned, perhaps while growing up, that relationships are things based on values like anger, power, fear, jealousy and so on." She then asked what values relationships were built on inside our jails; I took it as a rhetorical question. She then expressed her fear that going to jail might make it even harder for her community to teach those men, when they came back, how live in relationships built on values like trust, openness, respect and sharing instead.

I wish I could tell you how many times such simply-stated observations by aboriginal people (especially the grandmothers!) have shaken my professional convictions to the very core.

For the first time, I had an explanation for why so many people who were abused as children grow up to abuse children themselves; I could never understand how someone who knew first-hand the pain of being a helpless victim could grow up to inflict exactly the same pain on others. Under the relational lens, they were simply operating within the same kind of relationship they knew from their childhood, the **only** kind of relationship they knew of, a relationship based on manipulation, fear, lies and using others for self-gratification. The only difference was that they now held the position of **power** in that relationship.

It also helped me understand why so many of the offenders exposed to powerful healing programs were ultimately moved into a stage of explosive remorse: they had never forgotten the pain of their own victimization. In fact, it seems that a part of them recalled that childhood pain even as they victimized others, giving rise to intense guilt and self-loathing. Not knowing how to relate in any **other** ways, however, meant that they'd abuse again, and that their guilt and self-loathing would grow exponentially

Finally, the relational lens has drawn me towards a strange sort of proposition: perhaps the thing we feel as 'justice' is not really about 'stuff' at all, whether it is the criminal act, the physical loss or injury, the work done or dollars paid in compensation, or even the years served in jail in an attempt to somehow atone for what was done. If our lives are made precious by the relationships which nourish us, and if crime is understood as a disruption of those relationships, it may be that justice involves not only deterrence and community protection but also three **relational** goals:

> (1) having offenders come to understand, on an emotional level, the relational infections which their crimes have created in others;
>
> (2) examining the relational disharmonies in the offender's life which spawned the crime, and working towards different ways of relating so as to reduce the likelihood of its repetition; and

(3) searching for ways to move both parties out of the relational disfigurement that has bound them together from the moment of the crime.

I will start with the third, a proposition I never considered until recently: **each and every crime establishes an immediate, intense and unique relationship between the victim and the offender , an imprisoning relationship which will seldom alter of its own accord.**

E.   The Victim-Offender Relationship

I am just beginning to gain some sense of how unique the victim-offender relationship really is; I freely confess that I would have remained completely in the dark had I not been exposed to a number of different processes in which victims and offenders came face-to-face in non-court settings to explore all the issues between them.

First, it is a relationship which one party **imposes** on the other, against their will.

Second, its imposition is, most often, a complete surprise, coming in one shocking instant that was never anticipated. Even long-term grooming by sexual predators involves, at the moment of abuse, an instant change in the relationship the victim **believed** they had.

Third, crime-based relationships are **always** premised on violence or the threat of violence, and every dimension of them is colored by that threat.

Fourth, relationships established by crime are not organic, developing entities which modify over time. Instead, for the simple reason that victims and offenders rarely communicate except across a courtroom in silent, hostile stares, they are virtually frozen at the moment of violation. Unless significant, intentional effort is directed at changing that relationship, both offenders and victims will remain **locked** in it, with all of the violence, confusion, fear and mystery that it initially aroused.

Fifth, unlike other relationships, the parties who have become so powerfully linked to each other often have almost no idea who it is they are linked **to**! Even when victims have known the person who suddenly offends against them, the sudden emergence of violence prompts the conclusion that they didn't **really** know the person they thought was their friend. The question haunting most victims is: "Who **are** you, that you could do such a thing to me?". Unless they are given a chance to gain answers to that question, the likelihood of their achieving a gradual return to open and trusting relationships with others seems greatly diminished.

One dramatic case illustrates most of those propositions. It involved a young woman working at an all-night gas bar who suddenly found herself confronted by a drunken man barging in, threatening her, demanding cigarettes. She managed to sound the alarm and he was caught as he fled. The whole episode lasted only a minute or so, but his angry, threatening face made an indelible impression of midnight menace. She could no longer work at night, because every man who came through the door represented, for the first instant, his return. In fact, being **anywhere** alone at night was now a threatening experience. Her mother now constantly demanded to know where she was going, who she'd be with, where she'd park and so forth; despite never having seen the man herself, her secondary terror was so great that it was becoming a major burden on both of them. One crime, with no physical injuries, lasting no more than a minute, had severely impaired not only the young woman's relationship with her workplace and her city at night, but also their mother-daughter relationship.

Fortunately for both of them, they were given the chance to ask the "Who are you?" question - and many others - during a lengthy sentencing circle. They learned that the offender, despite sporadic acts of random, drunken violence and theft (for which he'd been imprisoned many times) was also a man who, during lengthy sober periods, had held good jobs in journalism. By the end of the circle, their fear had been so dissipated that they agreed that he perform substantial community service work **with them**, at the very gas bar he robbed, after he finished the jail sentence his criminal record required. Several months later, the victim appeared on an R.C.M.P. videotape to describe how important it had been for her, her mother, and the relationship between them, that she had faced him in the circle. Only then could she start to let go of the nightmare vision created by her first encounter with him.

As a side-note, having the offender's friends and families in the circle often helps victims see that the offender too lives within human relationships. Family members often have powerful stories of their own struggles with the offender's deteriorating behavior, and feel significant remorse for the harm done. When they put that human face on the offender's life, they contribute a great deal to helping victims see that their assailant was a real (though troubled) human being, not a creature of nightmare.

When the victim has never **seen** the offender, the "Who are you?" question is even more central. The teenager dashing through the patio doors to steal the bottle of rum is a good illustration. The victims couldn't put either a face or a body to the image they had of an intruder violating the sanctity of their home. Naturally, they imagined the worst. While they seemed somewhat relieved to hear that he was not a serial rapist, but a high school student with no criminal record who had spotted the bottle on his way to a party and given in to the impulse to steal it, the fear of the unknown remained. Even when they came to court to see him, to hear his lawyer describe his life, the unease remained. What they really needed was a chance to ask him the questions that I know were left unresolved, and to gauge, **for themselves**, the truth and sincerity of his answers: "Were you stoned? Angry? Was there some other reason you came in? How long were you inside? Did you look into other rooms? Into cabinets? Into drawers? Did you touch the knitting I'd left on the couch? Drink the water that was on the counter? What would you have done if we'd been in the living room? If we'd screamed? Or come after you?"

In every victim-offender encounter I've observed, there have been a host of "Who Are You?" questions that **only** the offender can answer. Many of them are not even consciously known to victims in advance, and don't emerge until the encounter is well under way. If they don't emerge, however, they never truly fade away.

I once heard Robert Yazzie, Chief Justice of the Navajo Tribal Court, say that the most important piece of paper in traditional Navajo Peacemaking was… the Kleenex! As he explained it: "Until I know how you feel, and you know how I feel, we'll never move *beyond* those feelings." The comparison with my own justice system is startling: as soon as a victim or a witness starts to cry, the court takes a recess to let everyone 'collect themselves' so we can then get 'back to business'. In relation-centered processes, hurt **is** the business.

I am happy to report that successful victim-offender encounters **can** significantly alter the victim's sense of relationship with the offender. The image of the remorseless criminal psychopath may be substantially replaced by the sight of a feeling human being, unbridled fear may be substantially replaced by realistic assessments of risk, and the power imbalance of the initial victimization may be substantially supplanted by a safe encounter between relative equals. Miracles are unlikely, and it may take many encounters over a lengthy period of time to achieve deep alteration if the crimes were deeply wounding, but the alternative - doing nothing whatever to alter the crime-inspired relationship - amounts to a virtual guarantee that victims will **remain** mired, often forever, in the relational disfigurements created by their victimization.

One particular case struck me very powerfully in this regard. It involved a young drug addict who supported his habit by breaking into houses and stealing things he could fence for cash. He was stoned on one of those break and enters, using a candle to light his way, and ended up setting fire to a house, killing a woman and one of her two daughters. The surviving daughter not only lost her mother and sister but was also robbed of her childhood and her opportunities for higher education, for she had to take over all the household duties. He was convicted and sentenced to 10 years in jail. In a process too lengthy to detail here, she participated in a series of letter exchanges with him, then videos, then face-to-face encounters. It changed her life to such a degree that she now joins him in making presentations to public groups about what those encounters have meant for both of them. She speaks about the hatred and fear she carried for so long, and the gradual release that came as they slowly moved into full exploration of the issues between them. They both needed those encounters because the crime was still ragingly alive between the two of them, imprisoning them in separate, but intimately intertwined, ways. It is her conviction that she would never have been able to move into a 'normal' life had she not been given the chance to communicate with him as she did.

Those encounters also affected **him** deeply. Because she was willing to face him, speak to him and listen to him, he felt an immense obligation to prove her investment worthwhile. As hard as it is, he frequently accompanies her to those public presentations, stands in front of many strangers, acknowledges over and over the horrible crime he committed, and speaks about how powerful and   painful - but ultimately freeing - it was to have to face her.

It took me many years to finally see it, but almost every victim has another question as well, one which **only** the offender can answer. I noticed it first in sexual assault cases, where victims frequently spoke about a lingering feeling of personal guilt, a deep-seated worry that perhaps, in some way they didn't understand, they might have **contributed** to their own victimization. It seems to exist whether it is a rape by a stranger or sexual abuse by a once-trusted adult. It continues long after the crime itself, and is expressed in many ways: "I wondered what was wrong with me, that he would pick me"; "I should have seen it coming"; "I can't believe I didn't do more to stop it". Most often, it simply comes out as a simple "Why me?"

And it's not just sexual assault cases which prompt such worries. Victims of all varieties of crime routinely ask "Why did you pick me? Was it something I did wrong? Was it something I didn't do right?" Those questions emerge even in property crimes: "Did you steal my gas can because of where I left it?"; "Did you break my windows because of something I did to you, or represented to you?" ; "Did you chose my house because that hedge I put in last summer gave you a place to hide?". I sense that it's more than a desire to know if there's something they might do to make sure it never happens again, that it springs from a deep-seated fear that there's something inside each of us that **deserves** to be treated in such a way.

Whatever the source, one thing does seem clear: most offenders are surprised to hear victims ask that question. Many seem startled that their victims would even **think** they were somehow responsible. When offenders show their surprise, and then answer that their selection had either been completely random ("I just picked the first woman walking alone who came around that corner") or based on criteria that had nothing to do with them as a person ("I dunno, you just had short hair, that's all "), the flood of relief is almost instantaneous. It is as though a thousand therapists could tell a victim "It was not your fault, you did nothing wrong" and it would not create a fraction of the release that comes from a single look of befuddlement on the face of their offender.

Another area of victim concern has to do with the **future** of their relationship with the offender: "Is there any chance he'll come after me again?" Victims gain very little comfort simply hearing the defense lawyer talk about the offender's remorse; they need the chance to gauge it for themselves. Some victims come right out and demand "Do I have any reason to fear you now?". Others come at it less directly, asking things like "When it was over, what did you think then? What are you thinking now about what you did?" or "Now that you've heard how your crime has affected me, has it changed the way you think about what you did?"

Surprisingly, it's not even the **degree** of risk that seems central, but the fact that victims are given a meaningful opportunity to come to their **own** assessment. It is, after all, **their** relationship, not the court's. If they assess it to be small, the relief is immense. Even when they conclude that a risk does remain, however, it is at least a known risk, one they can respond to, rather than an unknown risk haunting the edges of every day.

Crimes which cause death create even more intimate - and confounding - relationships. Surviving friends and family of the victim most frequently have no idea whatever about the events that lead to the death, what kind of person would cause it, what risks they face themselves - or how they should picture the last hours of the person they lost.

I recall a case involving the kidnap, rape and murder of a teenage girl. The father, mother and surviving sister sat through the trial, but it only gave them evidence tying the two accused to the crime. They still had no real sense of the full sequence of events that night, because neither accused spoke. The offenders were convicted and jailed for life, but as time went by the surviving family members, especially the father, found that their questions grew. Who did what to her? In what order? What did she say or do? Did she suffer a long time, or was it over quickly? What was the role of each accused? Did either of them try to resist what the other was doing? Did either of them show any humanity towards their daughter at all, or did they just revel in their torture? The father set up a series of jailhouse meetings with one of her killers and began to ask those questions. When I asked him if he could explain why he felt such a need to know each horrible detail, he answered without hesitation: "No truth", he told me, "could be worse than my imagination". While he had some chance of psychologically dealing with a known reality, no matter how horrible it was, he could never deal with a black hole. His series of in-prison meetings ultimately gave him enough apparently reliable detail that he could begin to 'move on' psychologically.

I encountered a similar dynamic in a case where one drunken young man rolled his car and killed his passenger, a close friend. The parents of the youngster who was killed needed to know about their son's last hours, where he was, what he was thinking and feeling, how the accident unfolded, exactly what the injuries were and how the driver reacted. They couldn't get those answers out of the courtroom, because the accused chose not to talk. As a result, they were left with an accumulation of unanswered questions that significantly impaired their search for a way to 'store' their tragedy and begin returning to their lives.

I don't mean to suggest that every victim or survivor wants to know every detail. I have had victims who emphatically wanted **not** to know each detail, at least at the time of trial or sentencing. As I became more alert to the possibility that learning more about either the offender or the crime itself might be an important part of victim recovery, however, I have broached the subject more frequently with victims, and a substantial number acknowledge a wish to know. Many seemed embarrassed to admit it, perhaps worried that we'd think of it as only morbid curiosity. Others found that their need to know didn't even show itself until long after the case was over, when they realized that they were not 'dealing with it' very successfully.

F. The Victim's Relational Disfigurement

I earlier mentioned the apparent need of many victims to tell their offenders directly about the impact of the crime. No lawyers please, no careful words to sugar-coat the message, just "Here is how your act has changed the way I relate to everything around me! Now, how am I supposed to get out of this, because I HATE being this way!"

At first, I believed that victims said such things simply out of a desire to 'hurt back', to make their abuser squirm under their anger. In some cases that may be the full explanation, but for many others there's another need, the need to make the offender **understand** what they've done. It is a message which becomes doubly powerful if friends and family of the victims join the circle, telling the offender about their own observations of change: "She used to always play after school, but now she just goes to her room"; "He wakes up every morning at 4 a.m., and I find him sitting alone in the dark"; "She doesn't even feed her dog any more". I've often heard victims complain "There's no justice here" and then add as their explanation "He has no idea what he did to us." It's as if they need to say "You imposed this relationship on me, and you need to know what it feels like from this end."

The case of the teenager who had been kidnapped, raped and murdered illustrates the dynamic. The father needed to tell that man what it **felt** like, morning after morning, to come down to the breakfast table and see that his daughter was not there. His surviving daughter needed the same (though to a lesser degree), to tell him about the huge hole in her world, now and forever, caused by the loss of her sister. It took many visits, many challenges to the killer's evasions, denials and minimizations, but one day they got through to him far enough that a tear formed in the corner of his eye. As I listened to them explain the process, my sense of what justice meant to them began to change. It did not seem to come primarily from the life-sentence which the courts imposed, although that was no doubt important. It emerged only after they had swamped him with so many stories of loss and deprivation that his hard face cracked and they knew he finally 'understood' what he had done, on the emotional level, where it really counted.

There are clearly categories of offenders where such encounters would be entirely inappropriate or even dangerous. I think here of offenders who are psychopaths with no **capacity** for empathy, or sadists who would take **joy** in learning how deeply they have hurt. It must be recognized, however, that those categories of offenders are rarities in the criminal justice system.

There are also categories of **crime** where bringing offenders together with their victims may never be appropriate, or appropriate only after lengthy but **separate** healing processes have been attempted.

I am thinking here especially of sexual assault and sustained domestic violence, where imbalances of power and levels of fear are likely to be extreme. In both domestic violence and sexual crimes between people known to each other, the issue is not just the imposition of an unwanted relationship but the betrayal of an existing one. Betrayals prompt such profound feelings of personal loss and menace that many victims recoil in horror at the thought of even seeing their abuser again, much less engaging him or her in conversation. I am familiar with some programs dealing successfully with the sexual abuse of children by family members, and they know from the outset that it may **never** be safe to bring those parties face to face.

If the abuse has been regular, the relationship may well be **defined** by its imbalance of power, and any encounter hastily arranged will only be a further manifestation of that imbalance. Offenders will continue their manipulation through abject apology, and victims will do exactly what they are conditioned to do, by appearing to accept that apology. Victims will seldom feel safe enough to even ask questions, much less articulate their pain; after all, telling their abuser how he has inflicted pain in the past is tantamount to detailing how pain can be inflicted in the future. Besides, many victims have not even admitted their traumatization to themselves, so conditioned are they to just 'carrying on'. In those kinds of cases, a great deal of individual work must take place with each of the parties so that each can learn how to move confidently within relationships based on openness, courage, generosity, listening and trust rather than the anger, fear, subterfuge, jealousy, manipulation and violence they have known.

That does not, however, mean that nothing can be done to initiate offender learning where abuse has been longstanding. I have seen several instances where an offender was brought together with a group of recovering victims of the same **kind** of crime. In some ways, these encounters with 'surrogate victims' may be the most powerful way to begin. Surrogate victims are often able to provide excruciating detail about how their lives have been affected, perhaps because they are not facing their own assailant. At the same time, it seems easier for offenders to **listen** to such detail when it comes from strangers, to let it penetrate, perhaps because it is not their crime being discussed. When it does finally sink in that their crime must have caused almost identical damage, however, the impact is often significant - and the manifestation of an empathetic reaction is often sudden and extreme.

And there's my segue into the other aspect of the victim-offender relationship: the needs of the offender.

F. Offenders & Justice in the Relational World

My experience with offenders strongly suggests that the vast majority have very little understanding of the true relational impact of what they have done. The youngster who thinks he 'only' ran into a house and stole a bottle of rum seems genuinely shocked to discover how fearful the householders have become, how they wake up sweating with every strange sound in the night. The purse snatcher who 'only' pushed his victim to the side and ran away seems stunned to hear that she is now too frightened to go anywhere alone, that she now looks at every strange man approaching her as a possible attacker.

In fact, most offenders seem to start with the proposition that the victim is making a mountain out of a molehill. It is my present view that, until they are forcefully shown the relational damage they have done, they will continue to minimize their behavior and resist any demands for significant change. They need to hear **directly** from everyone who was touched by the crime, including their own family and friends, without time limits and without glossing over the pain. Unlike the court setting where the focus is on facts and events, such encounters aim the spotlight at the emotional, psychological and even spiritual damage suffered by everyone touched by the crime.

My 19 years as a prosecutor tells me that the vast majority of offenders, while they do not understand what they have done, do not lack the **capacity** for empathic connection to others. True psychopaths and sadists are numerically rare in the criminal justice system, but it is sadly common to find people who have learned to tightly control - or even wholly deny themselves - any openness to the pain of others. Perhaps they simply felt too much of their own at some time, and taught themselves to shut down.

I was told of a case where a 'hardened' young offender met with an elderly woman whose car he had stolen. She told him that her husband had just died, that he had always done all of the driving, that now she had to do it on her own and had bought a special red car with the almost all of the cash proceeds of his estate. None of that seemed to penetrate very far. Then she asked why his father wasn't at the conference, he answered that he hadn't been a big part of his life and, besides, he'd died a few weeks earlier. She looked at him and said "So, you **know** what loss is, don't you". That incorporation of **his** loss, paralleling hers, brought tears to his eyes, and in that instant an empathic connection was established between them. They went on to both do special things for each other during his custody and, at least in the context of his dealings with her, the 'tough guy' had melted away. You have to start somewhere!

One of the keys for both parties in victim-offender exploration thus seems to involve getting to the point where they recognize that they are capable of feeling the **same** things. Perhaps its paradoxical, but that seems to occur most frequently when victims provide the most heart-wrenching and fulsome portrayal of their pain. The Cree grandmother would probably think it terribly obvious, but it's a relatively new thought for me: most offenders probably have experiences of victimization in their lives that are remarkably similar, at least in the **emotional** dimension, to what they have just caused the victim to feel. When they are prompted to **recall** their own pain, humiliation or fear, when their 'tough guy' exterior cracks and breaks in ways we never see in the courtroom, they have taken the first critical step towards re-claiming the capacity for empathic connection. I have seen offenders **overwhelmed** by a flood of their own suddenly-revealed confusions, sorrows and honest regrets. When that happens, it's as if a huge burden has been lifted: the burden of insisting to the world at large that they do not care, do not feel, do not need.

The sad reality is that most of the non-psychopath offenders I have encountered only adopted that stance, that fundamental lie, because they could no longer bear the pain of continuing to feel, need and care when their only rewards were abuse, neglect and denigration. I don't know how many times I've gotten reports on sexual offenders which described horrendous, daily violence between their parents as they were growing up: the image I was most frequently given was of little children huddling together in dark closets, hearing the thuds and screams and curses just beyond the door, each of them plugging their ears to keep those sounds of horror from getting any deeper inside. It is that image which explains to me how so many offenders may be somewhat empathic when it comes to laughter, **highly** empathic when it comes to fear, and apparently without any awareness at all of another's pain. They had lots of practice growing up. But it is nothing short of heartbreaking to witness an offender slowly brought to an uncontrolled sobbing which implicitly declares "I have felt precisely what I have caused you to feel, and I hate myself so deeply for doing this."

And, when victims see them showing that heartfelt understanding of what they've done, it often gives them a sudden and substantial release from their **own** pain; some have told me that they wished no further role in the court's sentencing, because they'd already gotten what they really needed.

Accountability within the relational paradigm, then, does not seem to come from the same place as accountability in the criminal justice system. It does not rely on the imposition of proportional penalties regardless of offender understanding or remorse. In the relational world, if accountability is attained, it is **emotional** accountability premised on deep and often life-changing remorse, itself marking the achievement of a healthy connection between victim and offender. Descartes proposed "I think, therefore I am", but neither crime nor healing seem to take place within our cognitive realm; for many people, victims and offenders alike, the better description of their reality may be "we hurt, therefore we pretend not to feel".

Offenders often report that facing their victims in such processes seemed to free them in some way, so that they too could move forward in their lives. Having met their own (or even surrogate) victims face-to-face, having listened to everything they wished to say, having had the chance to express and demonstrate regret - all of these were seen in retrospect as enabling in some important way. I think especially of the man who burned down the house causing two deaths, and his intense wish to 'do well' by the surviving young woman who had agreed to meet him and work with him as a man, not a monster.

And that takes us to the next step after accountability: healing. How does the relational lens shed new light on that challenge?

G. Victims, Offenders & Healing in the Relational World

The Cree grandmother, when she looked at domestic violence, saw not separated offenders and victims but the relationships which ensnared them. She didn't try to describe a particular man or woman, to put labels on anyone, to classify them as this-or-that *kind* of person. She looked instead for what it was in their way-of-relating that made them less than they otherwise might be. The question she asked was not "How can we change him or her?" but "How can we change the ways in which they **relate**".

Aboriginal people often speak about the need for 'non-blaming' justice processes. For the longest time, that seemed self-contradictory: wasn't that the central task of anyone's justice system, to allocate blame, to hold people responsible for their blameworthy acts? As I have come to understand it, while relational justice processes should aim at making offenders fully aware of the harm they have caused and fully committed to never repeating their crimes, they must avoid any temptation to blame the accused as a bad **person**. The duty is precisely the opposite: to convince offenders that they too have the capacity to engage in healthy relationships which bring only good to others. Most aboriginal healing programs intentionally refuse to use terms like 'the offender' or 'the victim', preferring instead to speak of 'people who have caused pain' and 'people who have been hurt', emphasizing that we are **more** than what we have done or what has been done to us.

There is a fundamental aboriginal perspective at work here which needs brief mention. The goal of healing is to achieve relationships **entirely** structured on values like respect, trust, sharing, caring, courage, humility and love. It is understood that no one ever achieves that perfection; instead, we are all on a journey **towards** that mythical state. Some of us start our journeys blessed with healthy experiences, skills, freedom from addictions and so on. Others are not so fortunate, starting their journey encumbered by fear, loneliness, anger and the like. We are all, however, on the **same** journey, and we can all learn and move and progress. Within that understanding, it is simply not accurate to say things like "I am well, you are ill"; the distinction between healer and patient loses its force, as do the boundaries between them. The sense that 'we are all on this journey together' seems to characterize most interactions - and gives offenders the critical message that they are not some lower order of humanity destined never to rise above their sins.

The healing question then becomes: what will help this person, whether victim or offender, move further towards health than they have been able to go thus far? At this stage in my exposure to aboriginal processes, I think I've seen a focus on four goals:

(1) convincing people that they are **not alone** in all of the discouraging, negative things they presently feel;

(2) giving people the **faith** that they too can ultimately move into relationships centered on positive values like trust, respect, openness and the like;

(3) giving people the **experience** of operating within relationships centered upon those values; and

(4) giving the **group within which the person lives** the experience of, and the skills needed for, turning the group relationships in healthier directions

Some illustrations are in order.

I remember, for instance, a victim's healing circle dealing with sexual abuse. Most of the healing team were themselves survivors of sexual abuse, each of them at different stages of their own healing. As in all such circles, everyone has an opportunity to speak to whatever particular issue is before the circle, in turn, as the feather is passed. They can speak as long as they wish, or not at all, for all are equals, with complete freedom to choose their own level of participation. The issue for that 'go-round' was how people felt about their own bodies after sexual abuse. That is when I heard those two women speak about still feeling so dirty that they turned the mirror to the wall or pushed their grandchildren off their knees.

As I listened to a full circle of women telling personal stories like that, I watched the victim. She began the circle curled into a huddled ball, her legs crossed and tucked, her fingers and wrists balled, her shoulders hunched, her head down. She looked to be barely breathing. As the others spoke, a very gradual transformation took place. It was as if she was exhaling for the first time in decades, breathing out, then in, stretching and straightening the smallest degree, taking the first tentative steps towards joining the others in the room instead of trying desperately to be as small and invisible as possible. She did not speak about her own abuse on that first occasion, but simply expressed her thanks for being included in the circle to hear the others speak.

As I later came to realize, a host of important healing steps were just beginning to occur with her. I suspect that most offenders, themselves products of the abuse they suffered at the hands of others, would experience similar reactions.

First, the stories which others told began the essential, but lengthy, process of helping her to believe that she was not a **freak** for feeling everything she felt. They too had once felt all those dirty, lonely, fearful things. She desperately needed to hear that, described in words and tones that resonated with all the secret screams and wails inside her. She needed to feel the 'normalcy' of her responses, as extreme and disturbing as they may have been. Obviously, it would take much more than one circle for that message to be fully believed, but it was a beginning.

Second, that circle, comprised of those women speaking so openly about their own days of abuse and fear, was a **safe** place, a place in which she could, when she was ready, say anything she wanted. The sad truth is that many victims and offenders alike have learned to deny, even to themselves, the full extent of their pain. To do otherwise, to reveal it to others, had too often resulted in those people turning against them, using their vulnerability as a weapon. In relational terms, they had learned to be closed, secretive and suspicious, for those were the lessons of their pain. In the circle, however, they are given the **experience** of relationships founded on respect, openness, candor, trust and caring, for that is how the healers relate to each other.

In that connection, I remember once remarking, after an offender's circle had been completed and he'd gone on his way, about how 'full of good feeling' the circle seemed to be, even when the offence had been one of serious sexual abuse of a child. Everyone looked at me quizzically, then opened a discussion which I now see contained the following propositions: How can you bring about openness if you are closed yourself? How can you bring about respect if you show disrespect? Caring if you punish? Trust if you ambush? Faith if you condemn?". In their view, the values you hope to teach must be the values demonstrated in the process itself.

I shudder to think of the values I regularly demonstrate during the course of a criminal trial!

Third, the stories in the circle stood as a demonstration of the **potential** of the healing process, for every person there had begun where that victim now sat. Their behavior in the circle, the kinds of relationships they now manifested between themselves within the circle, demonstrated that they had been able to move, however slowly, into **new** ways of thinking, believing, feeling and relating. If they could do it, it was indeed possible. I suspect that many victims and offenders alike have come to the conclusion that, no matter how **other** people might live, their world will always be mean, selfish, violent and … sad.

I also suspect that no one can simply tell them that it could be different; they have to feel it to believe it.

Fourth, every person's story made it clear that every individual had found their **own** way out of their pain, their **own** helpers, and their **own** pace. No one had the wisdom to tell another what they should and shouldn't do. Their stories were offered as encouragement and illustration, not instruction. What seemed critical about that message was its implicit statement that each of us, victim and offender alike, is **competent** to reconfigure our own life. It is a message that stands in stark contrast to the central message implicit in violence, whether physical, mental or emotional: that the victim is powerless, worthless and somehow **deserving** of the abuse. Again, I suspect that a therapist could insist on that competence a thousand times, and it would mean very little compared to hearing the same message from people who had been exactly where you were, and once believed, like you, that they'd be mired there forever.

Some of the healing circles I visited incorporated people who had themselves offended in the past but who had moved far enough in their healing journey to now render assistance They are seen as especially valuable in the rehabilitation of other offenders, not just for the empathy they bring, but for two other attributes as well. First, they are often quicker than everyone else to see how offenders are minimizing their crimes, hiding from their impacts, offering hollow justifications or excuses, blaming others for the choices they had made. After all, they once used all those strategies themselves; they are thus able to insist, in ways that others cannot, that they be shed. Secondly, their experience of the pain involved in having those defensive strategies slowly stripped away during healing gives them extraordinary patience; while they insist that progress always be made, they know how excruciating it is to finally acknowledge, especially to yourself, that there was no justification whatever for all the pain you'd brought to others, that the responsibility was solely yours.

At the same time, the fact that they once sat where the offender now sits, but have since earned a place as a respected and valued healer in the community, stands as a powerful motivator in itself, for it declares that it is indeed **possible** to put the crime behind you in the eyes of the community.

What seems essential, then, is that the circle be primarily comprised of people who have 'been there' in their own lives. They may be guided in the way they speak by a professional circle leader who organizes the themes and maintains process safety, but it is **their** stories which seem to be the magic ingredient. Those real, human, emotion-centered recitations are what convince people that they are not alone in how they presently feel, that they too can build a life of better feeling for themselves and everyone around them.

And it goes without saying that providing the experience of healthy group relations requires the presence of a healthy group. I often wonder about the kinds of relations operating within offender-dominated groups, and how difficult it must be to move them all at once out of the unhealthy ways-of-relating which have defined their lives thus far.

But the healing story doesn't end there. There is one more ingredient that is seen as essential in the most effective programs: bringing the family and friends of the victim or offender into the healing process so they can all create their own relational healing program together. Not surprisingly, this strategy is also a necessary manifestation of traditional teachings about the nature of Creation and our roles within it!

In my travels, I heard that many aboriginal cultures refer to Creation by a longer phrase which is often interpreted as The Great Mystery. While I liked the humility of that thought, I originally thought it a little over-drawn: even if we didn't yet have the entire universe studied, dissected, chronicled, mapped and named, I could imagine, especially with computerization, getting to that point some day. At least, that's what I thought when I saw the universe primarily as a collection of **things**.

Then I was given the plant-in-the-meadow teaching, and all the others that illuminated it, and I began to contemplate the meadow not as a collection of things but of ever-modifying relationships. At that point my expectation of ultimate 'knowability' began to break down. While the meadow might have only a thousand 'knowable' things in it, it had 1000 x 1000 relationships, all of which were in constant flux at any instant of the day, week, season, year and century. In what sense could that dimension of the universe be 'known' by mankind? Could it ever be known well enough to grant us accurate prediction? Or predictable intervention? Or would we always find there were dimensions we had never contemplated?

It is this base perspective that seems to prompt the determination to bring entire **groups** of people into certain stages of the healing process, whether friends and family of victims or friends and family of offenders. If there are problems in the ways-of-relating within the group, then the group itself is the only body that can ultimately design its own **better** ways of relating. Western teachings, by contrast, suggest that solutions are best found by professional experts like judges, lawyers, probation officers, psychiatrists and so forth, all of whom should come as disinterested strangers to each case. Collectively, they are expected to create (and, in the case of the courts, actually *impose*) their solutions on others, whether they support them or not. My Alice-In-Justice-Land brain can't help but ask how forced reliance on professionals promotes either a sense of responsibility or the development of problem-solving skills, but that's what we seem to do!

In the relational vision, the role of the professional is paradigmatically different. It involves creating and regulating respectful processes in which all of the parties to the unhealthy relationships can come together in open but non-blaming ways. It involves helping them confront and discharge incapacitating emotions like alienation, grief, anger, guilt, shame, fear and the like. It involves guiding all of them into using their newfound knowledge of the relational problems – and potentials! - that surround them to propose workable changes in how they deal with each other. And it involves making sure that the processes employed give each of them the beginning **experience** of relating in trusting, generous, open, humble and respectful ways. The hope is that they will thus become the authors of their own recovery with respect to that particular problem, and establish relations that will help them avoid, minimize or respond effectively to any new problems that come along later.

Family groups bring something unique to rehabilitative processes: a joint exploration of the family dynamics which spawned the criminal behavior. Aboriginal healers look with wonder upon processes where the offender gets to present fundamentally unchallenged descriptions of what he did, what was done to him and how all the rest of the world feels about him. Don't we all know that, even in healthy families, siblings will remember common events in very different ways, having taken very different meanings from them? And isn't it part of the empathy-growing curve to learn to pay **attention** to how others are experiencing our times together, expecting those experiences to frequently be different?

Similarly, family groups of **victims** make powerful contributions. They bring not only their heartfelt sympathy and offers of assistance, but something equally important: their own observations about how the victim is sliding into less healthy ways of relating to the world around them. Victims often seem surprised to know how much their friends and family feel they've withdrawn into silence and separation, and family members need to speak of how powerless they feel to draw them out again. Every victim, and every victim's family and friends, will have evolved unique sets of relationships before the crime, multi-faceted relationships of such complexity that it seems unreasonable to expect that a professional outsider, no matter how expert and experienced, will be able to understand them, much less manipulate them with predictability. It is the group itself which must explore its own strengths and weaknesses, then volunteer its own multi-dimensional responses to the healing challenges that face it.

The professional, then, becomes not an author but a process-provider, not a creator but a promptor of creation, not a prescriber of choices but the provider of a context in which healthy choices can be made. It is the non-professional healers, however, the other men and women who have experiential knowledge of the challenges facing victim and offender alike, who seem to be the real 'guides' in the process. It is they who help everyone else learn about each other, then begin to experience each other in healthier ways, to learn from each other, take inspiration from each other, design together and develop latent capacities for empathic reaction with each other.

And that takes me to the final topic, the one that always sits behind the notion of 'together' in aboriginal healing processes.

H. Spirituality & Ceremony in Aboriginal Healing

I don't for a moment pretend to understand the depths of aboriginal spirituality. It has to be experienced, and my experience will be unique to me. I do wish, however, to convey my sense of its origins within traditional world-views and its critical role in effective healing programs.

As the plant-in-the-meadow story illustrates, the world can be understood as primarily composed of ever-changing relationships of dependency, as all things are seen as essential to a healthy whole. That basic conviction drives a further conclusion: our relationships are fundamentally centered on dependencies, and human beings are not, as the western view seems to hold, fundamentally a collection of rights **against** others, but a bundle of responsibilities **towards** others, towards all aspects of Creation.

The sweat lodge ceremony teaches this view, dedicating each of its 'rounds' to prayers with various themes, whether caring for the young or the elderly or the health of the universe itself, or asking for guidance in carrying out our responsibilities to all of them. Each prayer sung in that dark, moist place is a reminder of the sanctity of those other beings, those other aspects of Creation, of the sacredness of our interconnections, and of our duty to act towards them with respect. Little meaningful distinction is drawn between creatures of the human, animal or plant realm, or with Mother Earth, for they are all our relations, and we owe each them a central duty of care.

Such ceremonial affirmations of connection seem to be especially important to people who have grown up in abuse, for they have often been terrified into postures of wholesale alienation from the rest of Creation. As I mentioned earlier, when their only involvement with others has come from being **used** by others, they often develop a deep-seated conviction that they are, in themselves, wholly without worth. To be told, especially within powerful ceremonies, of your intrinsic worth within Creation, and of the importance of your contribution to maintain its healthy equilibria, is to be given a precious gift indeed.

I saw this dynamic one day when I watched an Ojibway medicine man take his teachings into a remote aboriginal community wracked with alcoholism, family violence, sexual abuse and the criminal neglect of children. He spent the day in the gymnasium passing traditional teachings to those children. He told the girls about their special relationship with water, teaching them that the moon is called 'Grandmother', she comes in 13 cycles a year, her cycles determine the tides, and each woman has her own 13 'moon-times' or menstrual cycles themselves, and that newborns arrive with the breaking of their mother's waters, announcing the beginnings of new life, bringing hope and health and cleanliness to all. As he talked about all those connections, he also talked about the responsibilities they created for women to **protect** the waters, so that all those life-giving, life-sustaining relationships would remain healthy.

I had anticipated that any mention of **responsibilities** to those unrestrained and unencumbered children would provoke groans of resistance, but I could not have been more wrong. They were, by contrast, almost desperately grateful for being told that they were important somewhere, that they had roles to play, that they were part of something larger then themselves - especially something as huge and magical as the universe itself!

I suspect that many offenders have a similar sense of isolation from the meaningful world, seeing no role for themselves except for being used at the whim of others. The western world refers to this as a lack of **self**-esteem; I suspect that the aboriginal phrasing would somehow describe a lack of belief that they had any healthy **'role within Creation'** instead. Being a part of healing circles seems aimed at producing that health-producing conviction: 'I am as trusted, as worthy, as valued and as needed as others, just I am as confused and fearful and timid as others. We are all making our own ways, but we are all together on the same journey, and we are ready to help each other as we go'.

Clearly, that is not what most offenders have learned to feel. I find myself wondering, however, whether there doesn't remain a deep-seated yearning for visceral connection, especially with other people, a yearning that may even intensify as the possibilities for connection seem to be stripped away. My conversations with people involved in the treatment of killers often paint pictures of men who describe some kind of emotional explosion or release which only killing gives them. Some have apparently described it as 'almost sexual' or 'almost spiritual'. This is not my field, but I can't help but wonder: Do we all maintain a fundamental need for connection with others? What if the only connections we know have been within relations defined by pain? What if our own painful connections growing up in violence have caused us to shut down our capacities for receiving the pain of others, so that only the most extreme pain can penetrate the walls which, though we constructed them ourselves, we can no longer move aside by force of will? Will the only connection to others that is left open to us be the connection of **astounding** pain?

Is the human need for connection stronger than the need for it to be reciprocally **healthy** connection?

Thankfully, my experiences of powerful connection have only been good ones. Quite apart from events like being present at the birth of my three children (and **trying** to assist!), many of them have come within aboriginal healing processes where I went as an observer and found myself quickly a participant. My experiences with other people in healing circles, in sweat lodges and in other traditional ceremonies, gave me such a powerful, emotional certainty of intimate and healthy connection with other humans struggling through common human challenges that I can only describe them as experiences of spiritual connection. It was not just that we joined each other, but that we all felt joined to something much larger than our collective sum.

I know that the spiritual component of traditional processes goes much deeper than that, but I hope to have at least given some sense of the **direction** involved. The challenge seems to involve nourishing a conviction of healthy and meaningful connection in the hearts, minds and spirits of all of us, regardless of whether, in a particular instant of our lives, the world wants to describe us as a victim, an offender, a healer - or a supposedly disinterested stranger.

I. Conclusion

In case you haven't guessed already, I don't really 'know' what I'm talking about. I have far more questions than answers, and I am regularly faced with propositions that seem obvious to me now but never occurred to me before. To close, however, I'll try to summarize some of the propositions that currently attract me:

1) neither offenders nor victims should ever be labeled as such, but should always be seen - and presented - as people first;
2) the physical aspects of the crime, while they must be acknowledged, are primarily important as:
    (a) signals of the degree of dysfunction to be found in all of the relationships surrounding the offender; and

(b) the precipitate cause of dysfunctions now afflicting the victim in his or her relationships with community, neighborhood, home, loved ones, bodies, sense of self - or any combination of them.

3) it is critical that offenders be placed within processes that have the best chance of:

(a) bringing them to a heartfelt understanding of the true relational impact of their crime on others, including their own friends and families;

(b) prompting them towards an empathy-driven examination and revelation of the relational abuses that have been part of their own histories;

(c) helping them move past 'the worst their victims have to offer', by being given the chance to face them directly in a non-court setting premised on emotional exploration;

(d) giving them the faith that, over time, they too can achieve relationships based on positive values;

(e) giving them the **experience** of relationships based on positive values like openness, trust, generosity, humility and the like;

(f) teaching them to self-monitor the relationships they establish with others so as to move constantly in healthier directions;

(g) nourishing within them a sense of worthy connection to, and welcome responsibility towards, a **healthier** interplay of the forces that surround and nourish them.

4) the processes that have the best chance of achieving those goals are those which:

(a) require that they spend significant time with their own victims, or with 'surrogate victims' of similar crimes;

(b) require that all parties focus, in careful and respectful ways, on the emotional repercussions of their activities on others;

(c) require that they spend significant time with substantially healed **groups** of people

(d) bring in the other people involved in their web of daily relationships so that:

(a) their dysfunctional aspects can be examined by all and understood by all;

(b) the group itself can come to understand how powerful an effect it collectively has on each individual;

(c) the group itself can propose its own relational modifications, reflecting its own internal dynamics as well as the limits and potential of individual skills, strengths and capacities; and

(d) the group can start to develop the confidence that it is **capable** of making such changes.

(4) the primary healing will be accomplished through non-professionals bringing their personal stories of loss and recovery into the process in order that offenders (and victims) learn, in a human and visceral way, that:

  (a) they are not alone in their fears, pain, guilt and so forth;

  (b) they are indeed much 'more' than their criminal acts or their victimization;

  (c) there is no magic solution which someone else will design for them or provide them;

  (d) they must find their own ways forward, within their own contexts; and

  (e) they **can** find their own way forward, and begin to live in very different kinds of relationships, if they work hard and develop patience.

Of course, being a creature now dedicated to the pursuit of 'a good life', I will more than likely present a very different list five years from now!

Rupert Ross

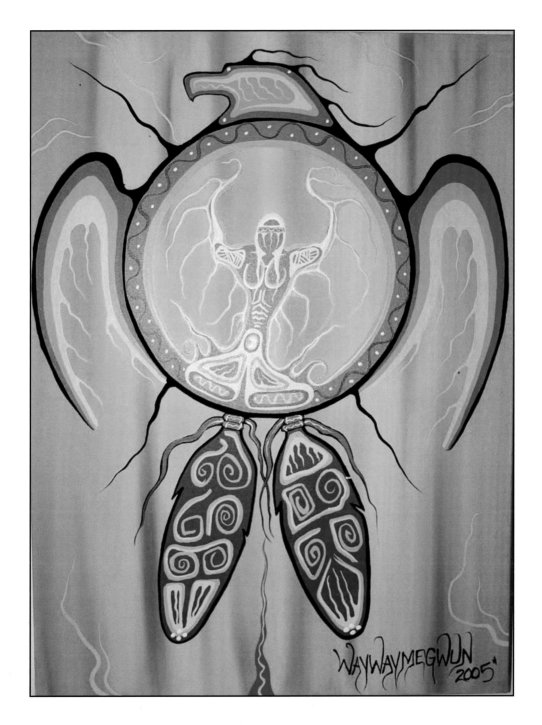

#52
"Beauty and Balance"

*Woman is the spiritual being who moves in balance
showing the beauty of one's soul.*

History of Conferencing

Our western concept of justice dates back to eleventh century conflicts between the church and the state. As each authority tried to expand its power over the people, the notion of law and justice gradually shifted from customary law, based on what people did, to a body of law which saw crimes as violations against the state. With this shift came an emphasis on the crime itself, rather than on the totality of the situation; the events leading up to the harmful behaviour and the subsequent ways of repairing that harm. As the concepts of justice evolved, victims gradually lost the right to direct their own cases. One of the ways that the Church did this was by creating a body of law, the Canon Law. Citing the precedents of Justinian's Code, the only ancient law code that allowed the state to prosecute, and not just mediate crimes, the Church radically expanded its power.

Canon Law not only gave a central authority the right to prosecute cases, but also to invent law as needed. Thus, laws could be invented based on abstract principles. As the Church, and later the state, began to prosecute crimes, the concept of wrong turned from the harming of an individual to a social evil. From these roots has originated a justice system that is focused on wrong, on rooting out evil, on punishment. There is seldom an element on how to make things right.

Justice has as primary purposes the establishing of blame and the handing out of a predetermined punishment. Howard Zehr refers to this focus as 'establishing blame and giving out pain.' Law students spend very little time studying the end result of the case, because the fulcrum of justice is guilt. Once guilt is established, we determine that they should experience some consequence. Therefore, justice is very authoritarian. Victims are left out and often ignored. Offenders are told what to do and what is going to happen to them... there is no opportunity for them to be held meaningfully accountable for their actions, no opportunity for them to understand the wrong and accept responsibility. In fact, our system reinforces the fact that, no matter how guilty you are, it's the government's responsibility to prove it. Therefore, perpetrators are taught to enter the courtroom and say "Not Guilty"... not because they aren't guilty, but because it is the state's responsibility to prove the guilt. Thus, we encourage the guilty parties to distance themselves from the actual event and its effect on victims.

As a society, we have allowed the public and private dimensions of crime to get out of balance. Crime has a community dimension and an individual dimension, that is, the harm to the victim. Unfortunately, we have elevated the public dimension and minimized the private dimension... there is no longer a balance.

The law is a blunt instrument. Once an offender is found guilty the options available are usually centred around shame and punishment even though research would indicate that these two consequences do very little to change behaviour. We stigmatize.

We say that the person who committed the crime is evil... what they did was evil. We sentence them to prison, but we never allow them the opportunity to remove the burden of shame. They will always be evil... always be an ex-offender. Therefore, we encourage these people to seek out other people who have also been stigmatized by shame. Now we have created, or at least allowed to be created, an offender subculture that is removed from the normal workings of society. And within this subculture, shame becomes converted into a badge of honour.

We have taken away, for the most part, the notion of personal and communal harm, and in so doing, have alienated all three components of the problem; the offender, the victim, and the community. A further outcome of that shift in law has led us to the misguided belief that the harsher the punishment the more likely the change in harmful behaviour. So we have taken a hard line approach to serious crime, and made that the norm for all offences - regardless of the needs of the victim and the community.

This direction in our legal system has also had a profound impact on our education system. Through safe schools policies and zero tolerance approaches to school misconduct, we have merged the two systems in a downward spiral of punishment and shame. Students who have stepped outside the boundaries of acceptable behaviour are now punished by both systems. They are given suspensions and expulsions from their school system and, in most cases, are also charged with a criminal offence. The problems are compounded by the fact that these two punishment systems rarely work together in providing any long-lasting solutions for the offenders, and they almost never look at the needs of the victims or the school community. There is no consideration given as to how to make things right again.

Often these days, discussions regarding school violence, safe schools, codes of conduct and the like, centre around a get tough approach with youth. However, strict discipline does not necessarily mean good discipline. The word discipline, from the Latin word *disciplina*, means learning.

In most schools, our notion of discipline has come to mean something far removed from learning. It has come to mean punishment, retribution and coercion. If we examine the consequences continuum used in school discipline policies, we find that most equate the seriousness of the infraction with some predetermined level of punishment. Moreover, these levels of school punishment in the form of detentions, suspensions, and expulsions have become closely aligned to the criminal code, thus merging the education system with the justice system for the purpose of punishment and exclusion.

Before we travel much farther down this path, we may wish to stop and examine the results of tough discipline programs in American schools. The metal detectors, the security- patrolled halls, the barbed wire, and locked doors have not had the outcomes that were expected. Rather than creating safe havens of educational opportunity, institutions of anger and mistrust have formed. Suspensions and expulsions have reached an all time high, and these youth, told they must now leave school, are creating havoc in their communities. The strict discipline policies used in the punishment of school violence may also, ultimately, contribute to it.

Let us return to the concept of discipline as learning and look at our education system, starting at the end results and working backwards. What kind of adults do we hope these young people will become by the end of their educational journey? Most would say that we wish them to become morally and ethically responsible, contributing members in society, capable of developing healthy relationships with family, friends and community. If that is our goal, then how are our policies, methods and practices going to assist them in reaching these outcomes? We need to examine the continuum of consequences we use in our school discipline policies, and honestly assess how many of these consequences contribute to the end result we hope to achieve.

It is not too late to change our direction, but we must first come to look at discipline with new eyes.

We must learn to live together as brothers
or perish together as fools.
Martin Luther King, Jr.

You never change things by fighting the existing reality.
To change something, build a new model
that makes the existing model obsolete.
Buckminster Fuller

Restorative Justice is a way of thinking about crime. It is a set of values and beliefs about what should be done when harm occurs in a community. It is a process which looks at the needs of the community, the needs of those who have been harmed, the needs of those who have caused the harm and ways in which all those involved can come together and find some solutions that will allow them to continue living together. The roots of Restorative Justice come from traditional teachings found in many aboriginal cultures around the globe. Much can be learned from cultures that focus on keeping the community strong, of giving everyone a voice, of respecting everyones' story, and of finding solutions that keep people connected with one another. The techniques of the circle process may vary but the values and principals of the process seem to remain constant and we can learn much from these teachings.

Community conferencing, which is an integral part of Restorative Justice, had its basis within the 'family circles' of the Maori people of New Zealand and the 'healing circles' of the North American first nations. These cultures believed that people should come together to help other people of the community. Everyone within the circle is given an opportunity to provide their own perspective, while being required to hear and feel the perspective of others. It is only when all members of the circle have spoken and been listened to, that healing can occur and the situation improved.

Though we often think that the practice of people helping other people is a relatively modern concept, in reality it has its roots in the birth of humanity. Cultures since the beginning of time have banded together when individual members needed help and direction. In fact, the case could be made that these native cultures have more effective emotional healing, teaching and learning systems than are now available within mainstream society. What is 'new' about our 'new direction' is that we are finally rediscovering the circle format of the ancients, and their emphasis on three areas: healing, teaching and learning. What goes around, comes around!

Australasia

Many victim-offender reconciliation or mediation programs came into existence in the 1970's, but had minimal impact outside of the small jurisdictions where they were practised. The key moment in the development of modern conferencing is generally agreed to have been New Zealand's 1989 *Children, Young Persons and their Families Act*. This legislation adopted and modified the Maori family circle for use in the national juvenile justice system. The effect was immediate and dramatic. The number of cases reaching Youth Court dropped significantly, while many trials were settled by way of a series of conferences. For the first time in modern jurisprudence, those most affected by crime were able to become involved in the process.

It was in 1991 that John McDonald, in his role as advisor on juvenile justice and youth affairs to the New South Wales Police Commissioner, brought the concept of conferencing and restorative justice from New Zealand to Australia. Working closely with David Moore, then coordinator of Justice Studies at Charles Sturt University, the first program of its kind was developed in the city of Wagga Wagga, New South Wales, meeting with significant success by providing dialogue between policing practice and social theory.

McDonald and Moore integrated John Braithwaite's 'theory of reintegrative shaming' into the design hypothesis of conferencing. Braithwaite, of Australian National University, identified as a key variable the extent to which ceremonies involving shame are designed to reintegrate people back into communities, or to stigmatise them. Stigmatising people has the effect of disintegrating communities.

By 1994, conferencing was spreading to other sectors of society. There was a significant shift from policing and juvenile justice into schools. Queensland began to run trial conferences within their government schools. At the same time, New South Wales widely used their 'community accountability conferencing' in education (to deal with incidents serious enough for suspension or expulsion, and where achieving fair outcomes consistently presented a challenge). A year later, New South Wales introduced the 'Reintegrative Shaming Experiment (RISE) for Restorative Community Policing' to compare the effectiveness of traditional court processing with the police-coordinated program of conferencing. By examining the prevalence and frequency of repeat offenders, victim satisfaction with the process, victim and offender perception of procedural fairness, equity in sentencing and cost, the 1997 report found conferencing clearly superior to court on *all* these measures.

Canada/North America

Restorative Justice in Canada has grown out of a number of different models. Our aboriginal peoples use healing circles, community peacemaking circles grew out of innovative sentencing decisions by Judge Cunliffe Barnett in 1978 and Judge Barry Stewart in 1981 and the Family Group Conferencing or Community Conferencing models which originated in the New Zealand and Australia. As well, the first victim/offender mediation program grew out of initiatives of the Mennonite Church in the Kitchener-Waterloo region of Ontario in 1974. There is an interesting anecdote related by Dave Worth, one of the key people responsible, on how it all got started.

It seems that Mark Yantsi, a probation officer, met with a few interested volunteers, policemen and crown attorneys to discuss a Pre-Sentence Report he was ordered to provide on two Elmira youths who had gotten drunk and vandalized 22 different homes and businesses in one night. He knew they could be sent to jail, and then put on probation, but it wouldn't help the people of Elmira deal with the fact that 'their own' had caused so much grief. So the group decided that it might help if the youths could meet their victims... all 22 of them. The judge, Justice Gordon MacConnell agreed. And so the perpetrators met each victim individually and agreed on how they would make restitution - sometimes with money, sometimes with work. And in the end, the youths were welcomed back into Elmira society. Instead of being an ostracized evil, they were able to learn from their experience and remain encompassed by their community.

Since 1974, victim-offender mediation programs have been adopted in many criminal justice jurisdictions throughout North America. In Canada, one of the largest programs is in Manitoba, where an organization founded by the Mennonite Central Committee, called Manitoba Mediation Services, handles up to 400 mediations per year.

School board sponsored Restorative Justice, had a somewhat later start. In 1995 Lynn Zammit of the CAPSS program in the Toronto District School Board, and Arthur Lockhart of Humber College's Justice Studies, designed their first school board training for Family Group Conferencing based on Dave Moore's and John MacDonald's experiences in Australia. The Toronto area training involved police, court staff, defence lawyers, crown attorneys, counselors, teachers, administrators, community mental health staff, graduate students, and community members. As well as working with the Toronto District School Board, training has also been conducted for the Toronto Catholic District School Board (through the offices of Art Biffis). Training sessions continue to take place for various police services, school boards, community agencies, children's aid, probation services and children's mental health agencies. Since 1995 over 100 circles have been facilitated, with a successful track record approaching 100%.   Restorative Justice Initiatives are now developing across Canada, taking many forms:

- Community healing circles
- Community sentencing circles
- Family conferencing and community conferencing

• Transformative justice
• Victim-offender mediation

Organizations such as the Church Council on Justice, Operation Springboard, the Mennonite Central Committee, St. Leonard's Society, Rittenhouse, the Department of Justice, the Royal Canadian Mounted Police, the Ontario Porvincial Police, Aboriginal Legal Services, continue to advance the philosophy and practices of Restorative Justice in Canada.

Our planet is starting to go full circle - back to the beginning of creating communities: gathering, sharing, learning, growing.

#53
"Inner Child"

They came to a place where spirits danced and lives were transformed. As they arrived, they lay down their belongings, the moment that had passed. Grey in color—their spirit flame burns low. Beneath the earth 2 bears watch, for they are the ones' who contain the medicine from the northern direction, above 2 spirit eagles guide the travelers along their journey. Beside them their inner child. They have come to reach back and nurture their inner child

Circles in Schools

In 1994, the former Etobicoke Board of Education (now part of the Toronto District School Board) implemented the *Community Alternative Program for Suspended Students* (*CAPSS*). The *CAPSS* program is designed for students from grade 6 to the end of high school who are under a long-term suspension of six to 20 days. It is a voluntary program, with a focus on anger management, life skills, conflict resolution, problem solving, academics... all with a strong commitment to family and community involvement.

During the first year of operation, staff spent a great deal of time learning about models and practices that had or had not been effective with these students in the past. Overwhelmingly, these students reported that punishment practices such as being sent out of class, lectures from school administration and parents, detentions, extra homework, suspensions, etc., had little or no effect in their overall behaviour at school. In other words, doing things **_to_** these students had little impact on their disruptive behaviour. This, in large part, was due to the fact that these students admitted that almost all these negative behaviours were impulsive. They did not consider either the victims or the consequences at the time of the incident. They had little or no idea of the extent of the harm they had caused to others. In fact, they often felt that they were the ultimate victims because they had been caught and punished for the offending behaviour. Most significantly, a large proportion of these students also identified that they lacked the necessary skills in anger management and conflict resolution to keep out of trouble if a similar incident should again occur. It became increasingly obvious that the program could not be part of the punishment process if it was to have any lasting affect on the negative behaviour.

If we consider the continuum of punishment in our schools, we have been creative in the ways in which punishment and discipline can be delivered. In fact, some schools pride themselves on the number of discipline options they use. A sample of the continuum:

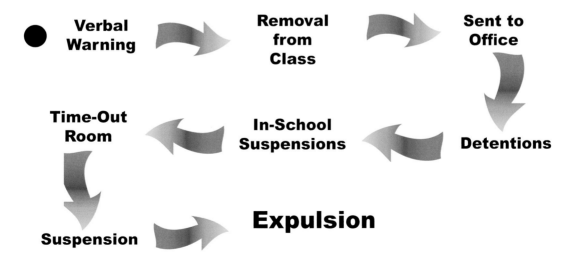

However, all these options still rely on the notion that if we increase punishment levels, if we stigmatize bad behaviour, if we remove students from their class at school, the bad behaviour should diminish. Unfortunately, for a growing number of students, this is not the case.

The *CAPSS* students were very clear in their understanding that increasing punishments would not have any significant impact on their behaviour, and if anything, it would probably escalate their sense of hostility and exclusion, in many cases leading the way into antisocial peer cultures where their negative behaviours and school absences would gain them respect.

These students were equally clear in what would make a difference for them. They recognized that they needed to develop skills and techniques in anger management and conflict resolution. Many requested assistance with their academics, many needed to build self esteem. A large proportion stated that they would like the opportunity to really tell their side of the story. Most felt the need to be more connected to their school community. They thought it might be helpful to sit down with the people they had harmed and talk things over. Many wanted to make amends. They all wanted to put the incident behind them and have a chance at a fresh start.

Gradually over that first year, the program took shape. It would not be part of the punishment continuum, but rather a new beginning. The *CAPSS* 'curriculum' developed out of leading educational research on building student capacities and the growing field of restorative justice.

In 1996, the *CAPSS* program integrated the restorative justice model of family group conferencing into the services offered to students, families and school communities. With the amalgamation of six former school boards into the Toronto District School Board (TDSB), we now interact with over 300,000 students in our system. In the restructuring of our service delivery model for at-risk youth, the TDSB has supported the ongoing development of a Restorative Justice Program which uses the family group conferencing model.

The Restorative Justice Program, launched in 1996, is a unique partnership between TDSB, Toronto Police Services and the justice system.

The conferencing process can address a wide variety of harm done in school settings including: bullying, harassment, truancy and criminal cases. The program goes beyond the usual consequences of suspension, police charges and expulsion. It focuses on the needs of the victims, the needs of the school community, and ways in which these needs can be met in a healing and constructive manner. It looks at what needs to be strengthened in that school community if such things are not to happen again. The conferencing model also offers a reintegration of the offender back into the school community with the supports necessary for success.

In 2000 the Ontario Ministry of Education brought into legislation the Safe Schools Act. As part of this new legislation, the government introduced strict guidelines for school boards in dealing with acts of school violence. Part of this shift included the creation of Strict Discipline programs for students who had been fully expelled from all publicly funded schools in the province. The act was a 'get tough approach' similar to ones used in the United States. The Ministry of Education funded a number of pilot programs throughout the province to provide research on best practices in dealing with students who had been fully expelled. One pilot project, the Choices For Youth program, located in the Waterloo Region District School Board, designed its service delivery model on the principles of Restorative Justice. All aspects of the program reinforce the notion of community, of repairing the harm, of skill development, of reconnecting youth and the success rate has been overwhelming. Based on this model, and the use of the Family Group Conferencing in dealing with school violence the Ministry of the Attorney Generals Office has awarded the Waterloo Region District School Board a three year grant to extend the conferencing model to all schools in the region as part of their safe schools initiatives.

The conferencing model runs parallel to the criminal justice system. It is not meant to replace the court process, but rather to take a school or criminal offence and turn it into a "teachable moment". The result is that youth are educated as to the impact their actions have had on others, they are held accountable for their actions in a meaningful and constructive way, and they are given the opportunity to make amends to their victims.

The Restorative Justice Program is now being offered through the four education offices. Facilitator training is provided through TDSB, as well as information sessions and workshops for communities, parents, police and agencies.

Without forgiveness life is governed by ...
an endless cycle of resentment and retaliation.
Roberto Assagioli

#55
"Mother"

It is hard to let go said the mother. And off their child went... With passion, un-conditional love, a mother watchers her daughter travel through life. Watching her reflection shining from within the beauty of the eternal child .

Restorative Justice:

When Art Lockhart asked me to write about the subject of forgiveness and its application to restorative justice, I reminded him that I retain a guarded optimism that restorative justice can work for some and a much less guarded cynicism that it could be easily misused. Despite this he asked for my written voice and so here it is.

As one who was a victim myself, I am not able to imagine my participation in a restorative justice circle for myself – perhaps because in previous encounters, my perpetrators showed no signs of accepting responsibility for their actions. However as a professional, I believe we must find better ways to engage alternative opportunities for victims and offenders to speak to each other, ways that are beyond our professional dependency on limited psychoanalytic processes. Processes that I believe as a professional have reinforced victim labels and client dependency on "the professional" for his/her healing. But beyond personal experience and professional training…as a member of the human race, I am afraid for all of us, if we do not attempt to understand and employ the complex paths of healing. One such path is restorative justice and its potential to provide some with healing that might not otherwise happen…and that can last a lifetime and beyond.

Janet Handy

Regarding Forgiveness

Janet A. Handy

Supposedly healing happens given enough time….

The phrases of "forgiveness" in "common" time sound like this…
    "Forgive and forget"
        "You have to forgive to go on"
            Not forgiving will kill your spirit over time…

The phrases of "forgiveness" in "eternal" time sound like this…
            Forgive seventy times seven
                Forgiveness is not yours to give
                Turn the other cheek

The word forgiveness is the most "unforgiving" term that there is. It implies no compromise, it holds no limit on time, and it will not vary in its goal.

It also tends to be a word "loathed" by victims, since many victims believe they should not have to do the work of forgiveness without their perpetrators also taking responsibility for their own actions. Victims do not necessarily buy into "forgiveness" as a separate state of mind or action. And therefore it begs the question "How do you forgive someone who does not believe they are in need of forgiveness". The arrogance of perpetrators has turned many victims away from the possibility of engaging in the work of forgiveness.

From out of my own experience of child abuse, to forgive my perpetrators was beyond my comprehension. In imagining the possible outcomes of forgiving my abusers, I remained focused on the perpetrators and their slippery evasion of responsibility. In the face of that evasion a resolve "not to forgive" rose up every time the possibility of forgiving presented itself and settled like cement on my spirit. I could not see this as my responsibility, nor could I see it as necessary to my "survival". In fact it often feels healthier not to forgive… because that too says I have a voice.

My journey to engage in the forgiveness of my abusers started on an adult level when I was in training for priesthood. How could I meet in a pastoral capacity with the perpetrators of others in jail for instance, hear their stories and offer forgiveness to them, if I could not accomplish the same for my own abusers. When I worked at Guelph

Reformatory as a student chaplain, I met up with many "perpetrators" of "break and enter" crimes, assaults and criminal behaviour that was a direct result of unleashed anger with no mechanism in place to contain that anger in the face of outside conditions of provocation, substance or alcohol abuse. Many were the human "products" of orphanage experiences and child welfare foster care systems.

These men…were they responsible for the abuse of others? – Absolutely "yes". Were they able to be on the street living reformed and violence free lives? - Probably not without first a massive change in reforms and the societal contexts to which these men returned again and again. And so was I glad that their rage was contained under lock and key? – "Yes" And yet, as I listened more and talked less, I heard the similar thread running throughout the patterns of their early lives.…

> In trouble at 7 years old – translated as "boys will be boys";
> In trouble at 12 - translated as "a short stint in reform school will knock it out of him";
> In trouble at 18, translated as "a criminal with no future".

Indeed the current stint in Guelph represented just one in a long line of encounters of rage mixed with a lack of socialization options, running into a legal system that is in no way integrated with support systems for mentoring or recovery from early experiences of their childhood abuse… abuse that is a part of a cycle of behaviours that 75 % of inmates have also experienced. No way out… therefore act out.

I actually found it quite easy to offer forgiveness as a priest, which many of them actively sought, at least in the name of creating the possibility of some spiritual level of peace. But I found myself having to consider the forgiveness in my own heart of society itself, for our profound abandonment of male children in general.

Did I however translate that understanding of the need for spiritual peace in the lives of my own abusers – No it did not help in that way. The wounds were too deep and the resentment too all pervasive.

My next efforts to forgive my own perpetrators of my abuse took the form of a theological search to understand the traditions of forgiveness…as taught in Christian churches. None fit:

> "…Forgive seventy times seven?"… Forget it… I don't have the strength;
> "…Turn the other cheek?"… No way …I would never survive that way.

And more popular reinterpretations did not work either. Such as 'forgive and forget" or "you have to forgive to be able to move on" etc. One thing that did help was to realize that the church does not include the whole and necessary balance in of stories in the bible when teaching from the lectionary (these are weekly passages set aside for reading during church services throughout the year and upon which sermons are often based). In fact, more often than not, these important balancing aspects of stories and biblical "directives" are pointedly avoided in sermon discourse.

I first understood the full impact of this omission when studying theology from a feminist perspective. The directive "Wives obey your husbands" was read and expounded upon at length in sermons, and further reinforced in wedding vows and was to be the general spiritual attitude adopted by good Christian wives. But the balancing directive, "husbands love your wives as you would your own bodies" was left unexplored. Domestic violence would be shameful if the second directive to husbands was equally emphasized from the start of a boy's life whether you agree with both directives or not! The phrase "children honor your father and mother so that your days may be long in the land your fathers have given you" was included in church teaching and in fact tied children, especially male children, to the legacy of successes or failures of their fathers in the world. This admonition, coupled with "spare the rod, spoil the child" meant that children could be beaten and yet they must honor their abusers, if they were to "inherit" their family legacy thereby remain in good standing and belong. But the balancing directive to fathers "Do not provoke your children to anger" was not included or unpacked for its intersecting impact on other directives. Parents were not taught to respect the emotions and impact of their actions on their children.

At this point in my journey to understand and achieve a state of forgiveness in myself, it hit me like a tone of bricks that my father was indeed guilty but so was the church in which he was raised, in which he was an priest by condoning in teaching and active denial the violence against my mother and the abuse of myself. The implications of these omissions were massive for me.

Did this understanding of the environment in which my father actions were condoned bring me any closer to forgiving him... still the answer was "No".

The next encounter came at a time, after 7 years of priesthood, when I was intensely involved in a review of my abuse experiences and coping with the present day impacts of the same on my relationships and vocation as a priest. After I had invested so much work in becoming a priest... I ultimately left the church, and renounced my priesthood, unable to cope with the church's betrayal of women and children's lives and now in my understanding, of men's lives as well. I also came out as having a same sex partner, something the church had deemed as perverse and sinful. I could not reconcile the Church's silence on violence against women and child abuse, with their active persecution of gay and lesbian committed same sex relationships. I was encouraged all my life to remain silent on the issues of violence. But then to be forced to remain hidden about what I believed was a freely chosen relationship was not something, as priest, I could condone in my spiritual engagement of others' journeys.

In this pivotal struggle for direction and meaning, I was often found myself in a mournful state of limbo regarding my professional and personal identity. I was drenched in pain and I found myself mentally "walking in circles" trying to make sense of all I had been taught juxtaposed with all I had come to believe. In this state of extreme wounded-ness I began to read more of the Old Testament and Jewish scholars. If I could only engage more ancient stories to find the meaning of forgiveness, (before the church took over the "dumb-ing down" translation of the bible's aesthetic storytelling powers), I thought that maybe I could still engage the spiritual dilemmas created in my life by not being able to forgive.

So in my own misery...I read the book of Job in his misery.... After all his troubles Job calls upon God to show "his" face and make sense for Job of all the woes and torments in Job's life, as Job has been a good and faithful servant of Yahweh and a "good and righteous person" to others - even to his enemies. But his friends keep saying to him… you must have done something wrong to deserve the torments you have encountered. A rather un-empathetic Yahweh appears in response to Job's cries and has a conversation with this lone and troubled human being, in which he says say to Job…." Where were you when I created the universe?"

The story itself and Yahweh's "answer" set everything that had happen in my life into a profound balance of inter-relationship with the universe and other human beings, which I had never experienced before. I can only say that at the time this story, written in this way "transported" me out of the my drowning pain, and allowed me to view my experience of personal pain, as connected in within a much larger picture of human grief and pain. I took profound comfort in this "story" of Yahweh, described as a vast spiritual entity encompassing the universe itself, was nevertheless speaking personally and directly to the one lonely and seemingly forgotten human life of Job… and yet the pain of Job is described by that same entity as only one small aspect of all that exits. Our pain is real enough to be spoken about, yet is but a moment in time, juxtaposed to the entire universe and its energy and creative genius. There was hope for my gaining freedom from debilitating pain and my limiting victim identity when that pain was put in perspective with the universal experiences of pain. Even now, years later in my darkest moments I re-engage this balance of my personal pain as it sits in the universe and I am able to engage my passion again to help others and at the same time self-soothe the wounds of my own pain. I believe if I had not found this balance in my thinking and spiritual life…I would not be here today.

Did this experience help me to forgive my father? No - but I found I could dismantle a part of that cement wall I had employed to fortify myself against any inclinations to forgiveness, with at least a small internal, reconstruction. I realized that my human frailty was part of the problem and that that frailty was not a negative weakness, as the church might teach, but a real consequence of being hurt. That it had nothing whatsoever to do with the will or lack thereof to forgive. I was weakened by my experiences as much as I was a strong person because I chose to live still. That weakened state had made life difficult to live fully but not impossible to engage. In fact like a person who is blind employs other heightened senses to override the unsighted losses, so too abused children override the experiences by creating heightened senses of imagination, fantasy worlds in which to live even while the abuse is taking place and yes unhealthy ways of coping too… all in order to find a voice and speak out. This frailty became my strength in that I could now consider that my father might also be frail, that he might also have wounds that could not be healed and that his rage was taken out on others less strong.
But it stopped there. I could go no further.

The latest part of this journey was in studying the Jewish understanding of what must be in place for "forgiveness" to actually be realized and not remain in the realm of just words. It is this…in order for forgiveness to truly occur… both the victim and the offender must make a complete turn around – a full 180 degrees of change; the victim in his/her attitude toward the offender as unforgivable and the offender in his/her reluctance to take complete responsibility as a free person for individual actions of abuse. In other words, in order to achieve true forgiveness between them they must be prepared to give up the previously held positions of victim and offender. The victim must be free of the anger and resentment that maintains the victim identity and instead consider the possibility that a victim has both the power to speak and the power to forgive another. Likewise the offender must be totally free of rationalizations, indeed even accepting that an abusive childhood does not excuse the damage he/she has caused another, thereby becoming a free person able to accept responsibility and act differently to change the cycle of violence against others.   In other words … is open to both receiving and being forgiven. Think about it – a domino effect of forgiveness…think of the work involved… but think also of the possibilities.

Daunting isn't it? I believe in our heart of hearts, that to stop war, stop hatred, stop hurting each other, cherish the universe and our place in it, that we as a collective humanity do glimpse even if only fleetingly, the work involved in achieving this 180-degree turn. And we also know that this kind of forgiveness can only be engaged if every single human being is are involved in what seems like this extra human effort.

Did this new understanding allow me to move beyond just considering forgiveness and into action? Not yet …but for a while it did allow me to understand that I was unable to forgive my abusers on my own and to at least give up carrying the worst of my anger and resentfulness alone instead choosing to "put it out to the universe" so to speak. This is some relief and in terms of my father…he died 26 years ago, so he cannot engage this other half of the 180-degree turn around. And the other circle of my abusers, operating within the church when I was a child… they were disbanded years ago, after an unplanned public exposure of their abuse of others. They remain unchallenged for their actions. But I continue the pursuit of forgiveness's meaning for the sake of the health of my own soul, for continued professional growth and social reconnection to the human race and universe within which we live. And when it is safe to do so, I grieve still.

JH5/25/05
From "Working Underneath": an Autobiography, by Janet Handy (in progress)

The Journey of Forgiveness

Rev. Dale Lang

Before our son Jason was shot and killed in his high school in 1999 by a 14year old boy, I would have told you how important forgiveness is, because as a Christian Pastor I knew something about it. At the Memorial Service for Jason, I did offer forgiveness to the boy who killed our son.

It was not until three months later, when the angry mother of a daughter killed by a drunken driver said she could not understand our family's forgiveness, that I truly began to understand forgiveness. When Jesus gave me the grace to forgive the boy who killed Jason, He set me free from being trapped in the place that angry Mom had lived for several years.

When we stay angry at the people who have hurt us, we are trapped. For if we stay in the place of anger long, it becomes very much like a prison: a place that is difficult to leave, a place that continues to damage us. When I stay angry at being hurt, I build walls. I don't want anyone getting to close because they may hurt be again or try to convince me to give up my anger. When we choose to forgive those who have hurt us, the walls begin to comedown. It is then, and only then, that it becomes possible for God to begin healing the wounds that we have received. Forgiveness is a place of healing and freedom. In the world we live in, we all get hurt and we will all need to forgive. Forgiveness is simple to define: when we can think about or look at someone who has hurt us, and still be at peace, we have arrived at the place of forgiveness.

This is not to say that forgiving is easy. It is often a difficult path to choose, but we can choose it even if it takes some time to arrive. Just choosing that path sets in motion the opportunity for healing. One note that we need to add. Choosing to forgive is not permission for people to abuse us repeatedly. Abuse needs to be stopped. Forgiveness does not mean that we are in anyway justifying wrong actions. It will never be right that our son was killed. But with the Lord's grace, we are so Thankful as a family that we could forgive and move on with life.

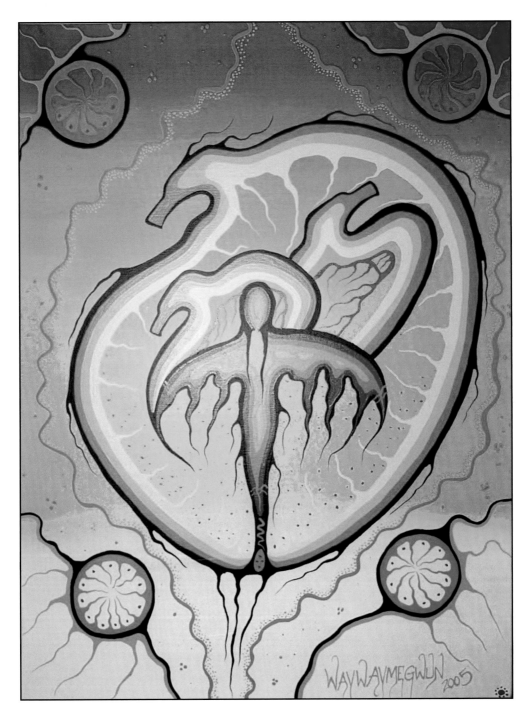

#56
"The Way"

There are those who speak through me. The cardinal points us to the directions where all spirits live. The ones' that speak in silence look within to look without. You can hear them talk. It is through me, through you that we are shown the way.

Education Theory:

IMPLEMENTATION CONTINUUM

Prevention
- violation of school rules and codes of conduct;
- elementary and middle school role plays;
- sports teams violations;
- conflict resolution model delivered through guidance programs;
- community issues.

Discipline
- pre-suspension, pre-expulsion incidents;
- pre-charge incidents, extrajudicial measures;
- serious discipline violations which warrant suspension or explusion;
- first offenders or repeat offenders;
- admission to a new school setting;
- community issues.

Criminal Offence
- level one and level two offences which warrant suspension, expulsion and criminal charges, extrajudicial measures or extrajudicial sanctions;
- first offenders, repeat offenders;
- diversion / alternative measures;
- pre-sentence report;
- probation;
- sentence (disposition);
- re admission from suspension or expulsion, or custody setting;
- admission to new school setting.

Conferences Co-ordinated by
- teacher;
- administrator;
- social worker;
- guidance counsellor;
- youth worker;
- suspension/expulsion program staff;
- police (in some cases).

Education Theory:

MODELS OF JUSTICE

Retributive Model	**Restorative Model**
• violent act violates policy/statute/code of conduct;	• violent act violates people/ relationships/school community;
• focus on the offence;	• focus on the obligation of offender to make amends;
• punishment decided externally;	• plan for reparation of harm decided by those affected by the incident;
• offender is defined by deficits;	• offender is defined by capacity to make reparation to the victims;
• focus on offender and incident;	• focus on victim and reconciliation of all parties;
• focus on removal of offender from school and community.	• focus on re-integration of offender with necessary supports.

All that we are is the result of what we have thought.
The mind is everything. What we think we become.
Buddha

Organizational Structure for School Boards:

WORKING IN PARTNERSHIP

An enemy is one whose story we have not heard.
Gene Knudsen Hoffman, Quaker

Organizational Structure
for
School Boards:

CONFERENCING FLOW CHART

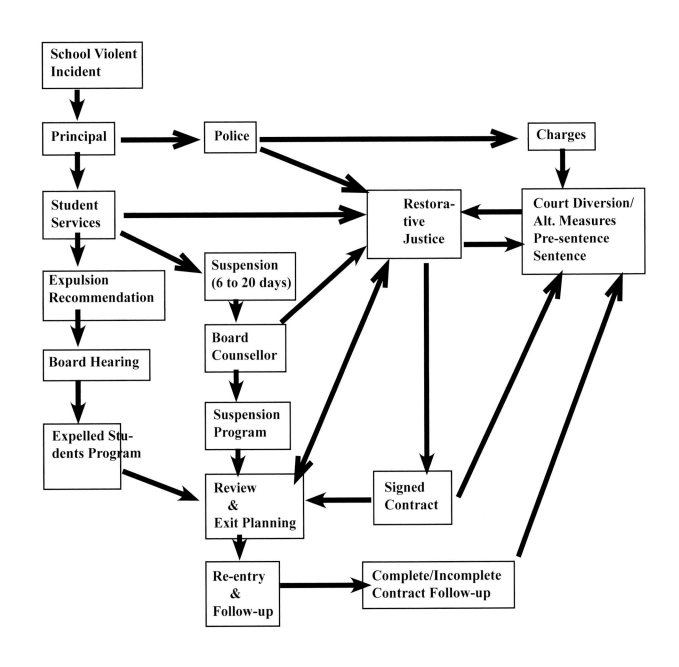

Conferencing in Schools

Over the last few years we have taken a get-tough approach to school violence, and many school boards have created strict discipline policies and procedures that reflect this trend. Police are being called into our schools more often, students are being suspended and expelled, and still the problems seem to be growing. A vicious circle is being created in our educational system... the more we try to control and punish, the more our students lash out and cause harm. With diminishing funds for guidance counselors and social workers, and an increasingly heavy workload for classroom teachers, we have an atmosphere in which our only recourse for harmful behaviour seems to be removing the offending students from our educational system.

As is often the case, our solution has created a whole new set of problems. When we disenfranchise youth from their schools we are merely moving the problem out into the streets and in to our communities. The problems don't go away, they just resurface somewhere else, and often the harmful behaviour multiplies as a result of our unwillingness to make meaningful changes in the way we deal with school violence. Our role as educators does not stop when our students act out, in fact, our role should increase. The justice system has a clear mandate to uphold the laws, as educators we have a clear mandate to educate our youth. It is in our best interest as a society to work together to do both.

This philosophy of exclusion does little to address the underlying causes of school violence and inappropriate school behaviour. It does little to address the needs of the victims and it offers no solutions for avoiding similar issues in the future. Rather than viewing punishment and exclusion as the only options we may want to redirect our efforts towards lasting change, towards skill building, towards rebuilding relationships and a sense of community.

We must ask ourselves the question: "If punishment wasn't an option, what would we do?"

This question may lead us into a very different direction. . .

Harassment - A Story

A number of teenage girls had been harassing and bullying two other girls in the school. The victims had gone to the school administration on a number of occasions to report the bullying but nothing had been done. One day while sitting in the school cafeteria, the two girls started to write out a "hit list" of people they wanted to harm. The list included the bullies but also included others in the school that had in some way displeased them over the last few months. They also included students they didn't like because of differing tastes in fashion. Friends walking by that day commented on the list and made jokes about who was at the top and how you could move up the list. There was never any intention to cause harm to the people on the list, it was merely a way to blow off some steam. At the end of the period the list was shoved into the bottom of a purse and forgotten.

Some months later, while at a party, one of the list writers had her purse search by another student without her knowledge. The old list was found and was subsequently photocopied and passed out to all those whose names were on the list.

The school administration learned of the list and called police. The two girls were taken to the police station, charged, stripped searched and thrown in jail over night. The school decided to expel the students who were both at the end of grade 12 and on track to graduated in June. As one of the girls was 19 at the time, her name was published in the local paper and as a result she was laid off from her job until she could complete a full psychological exam to prove she wasn't a danger to society.

The list, in a post- Columbine atmosphere, caused the media to run front- page stories on the arrests. The school spent weeks answering calls from concerned parents and students. The peer groups of both the accused and the girls on the list kept the tensions high and school officials could not seem to calm things down.

Finally, the principal called and asked if some kind of restorative approach might be able to resolve the ongoing tension in the school. I met with students on both sides and we had some long conversations about what had happened and the ongoing harm even though the girls were no longer in the school. The students felt that a meeting with all of them together in one place would be the only way to resolve the issue. I contacted the crown and she gave permission to proceed with a conference.

The conference participants included the two girls and their mothers, a number of students from the school, the vice principal as well as three girls whose names had been on the list.

When the two offenders talked about the incident and the impact it had had on their lives all the participants became very emotional. It began to hit home how large a punishment the two girls had had to endure.

They had been charged, strip -searched and left in jail overnight. They had both been expelled from their school. One girl had enrolled in another high school but because her name had been in all the headlines she couldn't escape the shame and humiliation. The other girl couldn't face a new school so had been working on credits independently. Both girls had been set to graduate in June but would no longer be able to do so. As luck would have it the day of the conference was also the day of the prom. Many of the students on the list chose not to attend the circle because they had made hair appointments for early in the day. Those that came announced that they would have to leave by a certain time so that they too could get ready for the big night.

Both girls had booked a vacation over March break with some friends to celebrate the end of high school. They had already paid for the trip and so when the police arrested them they had to cancel their trip and lost the money.

The two girls had been best friends for years and they spoke about how isolating it was not to be able to see or communicated with each other for months. Most of the time they just sat at home alone. When they were with friends the companions had to choose between the two, as they could not be together.

The 19 year old had been laid off from work and had to pay for a psychological assessment in order to prove that she was not dangerous before the company would reinstate her.

Both the girls and their mothers spoke about the original bullying that had taken place and how frustrated they were when school officials had not acted on the information. Certainly the mothers were, in hind -sight, upset with themselves for not pushing this issue with the school board at the time. Both families were under a lot of financial pressure because of time off work and the expense of lawyer's fees. They also felt humiliated by all the publicity and felt that the community had judged them as bad parents because their daughters had been involved. It seemed that no matter where they went in the community people were talking about it and the shame all of them felt was, at times, overwhelming.

One mother spoke of how powerless she felt when the police led her daughter away that night. As she said: "From the time I gave birth and the doctor put my little girl on my tummy I vowed that I would always be there to protect her from harm. On that night I could do nothing to help her. I just had to let her sit there in a cold dark cell and I could offer her no comfort or support."

The girls on the list had little to say about the original bullying except that it had all started over a boy. As they listened to the two accused, the girls who photocopied and distributed the list began to cry. The two accused thanked the victims for attending the circle and recognized how hard it had been for them. They apologized for writing the list and assured everyone that there had never been any intent to follow through with harmful actions.

In the end, when asked what they needed to see happen in order for the harm to be repaired, the victims requested that the conferencing contract instruct the crown of their wish to have all charges dropped. They specifically wanted the co-accused to be able to have contact with each other again. The vice principal stated that the school felt that the two girls had taken complete responsibility for their actions. The VP even offered to have the girls attend the prom that night but because of the bail conditions they were not permitted to.

The final reconciliation – one of the mothers of the accused invited all of the girls to a BBQ at their house in August when the court decisions would be complete.

There were lots of hugs and tears at the end and many of the participants asked why a circle couldn't have happened sooner.

A good question indeed.

This question may lead us towards a very different horizon.

Towards
A Restorative Curriculum

In the last 15 years there has been a surge in educational research into how students learn. Overwhelmingly this research points to the fact that we learn from the inside out. We bring to the table our past experiences, our emotions, our goals for the future, our fears and our own unique way of perceiving the world. It is in the areas of emotional intelligence, learning styles, metacognitive skills and other research that we begin to understand how we learn, how we interact with others... how we, as human beings, need to build communities of caring. The overwhelming results from this body of research indicate that there is a whole other curriculum - curriculum of the self - that needs to be taught in our schools. This curriculum serves as the basic building blocks for how we live and work together, how we respect each other, how we solve problems, how we communicate. It is in this body of educational research that we may find the answers to school violence. But we must be open to the teachings.

It is not surprising that in this new self curriculum there are themes that surface in much of the research. In *The Resilient Self*, (Wolin and Wolin) the authors have identified seven resiliency factors that are indicators of how well humans can overcome adversity in their lives. These resiliency factors include relationships, independence, insight, morality, initiative, creativity and humour. The research promotes the idea that these resiliency factors can be taught in order to overcome the difficulties we face in life. *Emotional Intelligence* (Goleman) outlines the core of this social and emotional learning by emphasizing the need for schools to teach a curriculum that focuses on emotional awareness, empathy training, communication skills, and relationship building, to name but a few areas.

There is a wide body of research that demands that we rethink what our students need to know. It is often argued that this new curriculum would take up too much time, that it would take away learning opportunities in regular subject areas, but doesn't classroom discipline also take up much of our time? If our students do not learn the social and emotional skills they need, they may not be in school long enough to learn the subject content.

In a restorative curriculum the emphasis is placed on building students' capacities. The emphasis is on understanding of self and others and the ability to build positive healthy relationships. Rather than viewing misbehaviour as a violation of school rules we need to see it as a violation of relationships. Violence creates obligations between people; we need to teach students how to make things right again.

By using a restorative approach to school violence we build capacity in our students. They begin to understand not only their own feelings and actions but also those of others. When we take a violent incident and turn it into a teachable moment, we create the capacity to change... when we use it as an opportunity to punish, we create something quite different. A restorative model also takes into consideration the needs of those who have been harmed by the incident. It not only gives them a voice in the outcome, it helps them gain some understanding of why they became involved in the first place.

Lastly, it allows school staff to do something more that just punish. It provides them with a tool to rebuild school community.

Ideally, all students should be taught the social and emotional curriculum. But often it is not until violence occurs that there comes a need to do something. In the aftermath of crime and violence there can be a place for healing and change. The Restorative Justice Family Group Conferencing Model allows this to occur. It is the perfect vehicle to start teaching communication skills, problem solving, empathy training, responsibility, and community relationships. The model gives the victim a voice, it holds the offenders meaningfully accountable for their actions and it gives them a means to make amends. Furthermore, it helps us look at what needs to be done, and what needs to be strengthened, so that this kind of thing cannot happen again.

Conferencing allows us to examine our notions of community. It allows us to break down barriers between people, it allows us to work together to rebuild a "we" attitude. When we build community capacity in our schools, when we use a restorative approach to violence, we emphasize learning over punishment and reintegration over exclusion.

Assault - a Story

A school in north Toronto had had 4 false fire alarms one Friday. When the alarms sounded for the 5th time during the rainy afternoon the school had to be evacuated yet again. As the firemen entered the building, a number of staff and students stood under the front porch. The first fireman opened the front doors and walked into the glassed double door entrance. A student followed him inside and a fight took place that left the fireman in need of a hospital stay.

The police were called and the student was arrested and charged. Several other youth had joined in the fight but could not be identified. The fire dept. was furious about the attack. The principal was trying to do damage control and the news media jumped on the story for the 6:00 news. The media portrayed the school as being in one of "those" neighborhoods with a high crime rate, gang activity and Ontario housing.

The following day the community was up in arms about the coverage they had received, the school's reputation had severely suffered and the conflict escalated throughout the day. The local trustee heard that the fireman had also hit the boy and thought that the accused should counter charge. The fire dept. wanted to charge the school board for fire safety violations because they had not cleared out the school properly.

During the next few days the fire dept. received numerous false alarm calls to the area and when trucks arrived they were pelted with bottles and stones from rooftops.

One board official, aware of our conferencing project, asked if this case would be one suitable for conferencing. Since the situation was escalating daily it sure seemed like it was worth a try.

I spent a couple of weeks interviewing all of the circle participants and then set the date for the conference. Participants included the student and his mother, head of the student council, a community rep, the fireman and his division chief, police and the principal and vice principal of the school.

There were a number of issues on the table: the actual physical assault of the fireman, the fire safety regulations that the school broke, the community response to the media coverage, the school's reputation and the 911 false alarms in the community.

As participants began to share their stories some interesting things began to happen.

The young man told of how he was standing outside the front doors when the fireman entered the building. As the fireman opened the first set of doors one swung back and hit the young man in the head (witnessed by the teachers standing outside with him). He proceeded to enter the building and confronted the fireman about getting hit. The fireman responded to the swearing by grabbing the youth by the throat and pushing him up against a wall. When the youth's friends witnessed this they entered the building and joined the fight. The fireman was pulled off the youth and pushed to the ground and repeatedly hit.

Once the fireman heard the youth's story he began to apologize. He had had no idea that the door hit the young man. The two main participants that day resolved their conflict in the first few minutes of the conference. The bigger issue that emerged, however, was that the fireman was furious with the school principal because he had never phoned to check on him while in the hospital. The principal stated that he was told not to make any contact by the board's lawyers in case the situation proceeded to litigation. It was evident that much of the harm caused has to do with broken relationships and harm to the larger community. The community rep heard about the false alarm calls and the student council talked about the damage to the schools reputation as well as the media stereotypes.

As a result of the circle process the following plan emerged: the student would write a letter of apology to the fire dept. and he would get help with his writing skills by the student council head. At next appearance, a copy of the restorative justice contract would be presented to the crown and the police officer would speak to the outcomes of the conference. The fire dept. agreed to come in to the school and run a series of assemblies about fire safety so that the student body would understand the dangers of false alarm calls. The student council and fire dept. agreed to work on a fund raising event together at the school with all funds being given to a charity program at the local community center.

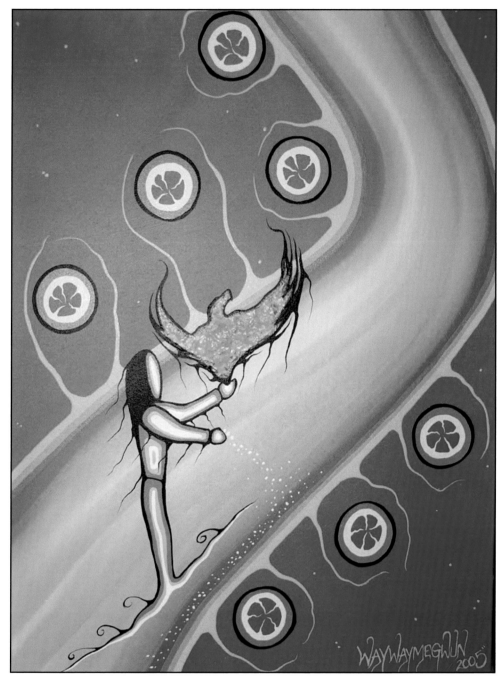

#24
"Lighting Your Path"

With eagle in hand, he lights the way by defining the capacity to see beyond, to know balance in the strongest of storms and able to soar in gentleness along the sacred path. As his footsteps are left behind he must also lay down the heaviness that impairs his travel along the sacred path.

It is in traveling along our sacred path that we find the 7 teachings: love, respect, truth, honesty, humility, bravery, and wisdom. When we forget to honour these teachings in our lives, they will move on and disappear from our path. It is our responsibility to gently embrace these teachings in order to travel along our sacred path with passion.

Community Building

There is a house located at 3101 Lakeshore Blvd, Etobicoke, Ontario. It is a house that, until three years ago, had all but fallen into total disrepair... not occupied in any meaningful way for over 30 years. It was boarded up, without hydro or plumbing. Rodents lived in its walls and rafters. It was a very visible and neglected "eye sore".

One day, I was sitting with a young woman in my car, across from the old house. The woman was telling me a sad story of having been abused and assaulted at gunpoint. The story was unfolding in the car because there was no place the young woman felt comfortable enough to talk. As she summoned her courage and continued the tale, I looked at the old house. I began to think that the house, if brought back to its original splendor, would be an ideal place for any young woman to come and feel safe... and to have her voice heard.

So the effort began. It turned out that the house (called the Gatehouse) was the property of the City of Toronto, Parks Department. A deal was made whereby it could be leased for $200,000.00. Of course I did not have $200,000.00 dollars, but the lease was arranged with the provision that any renovation costs would go towards the lease. I phoned some friends and they phoned some friends and pretty soon a community meeting was held. Everyone agreed that such a safe place was needed. The challenge was to rebuild the house, paying for the lease through renovation costs.

As the number of volunteers grew, each was asked a question: "what is your gift, your capacity, that you would like to contribute to the rebuilding of this house?" With this question the magic of community capacity building came to life. People had skills in project management, carpentry, electrical, construction, marketing, and fundraising. In six months, a house that had been neglected and abandoned for over thirty years, was transformed into a safe home for abused children, youth and adults. Today, the house has three fulltime staff, has helped over 4,000 people, and continues to flourish. All through the spirit of community capacity.

There is a parallel between alienated youth and the 'Gatehouse'. All too often, youth in conflict find that they don't fit in, that their potentials are pushed aside and under-valued. They are often segregated into special compartments, or have nothing specific offered to them. They become the "OTHER", looked upon as liabilities that drain resources. Seldom do we examine the potential and the unique possibilities that are presented. Seldom do we look at youth in conflict as people who have the capacity for personal trasformation.

Scott Peck. M.D. in his book *The Different Drum: Community Making and Peace*, opens his discussion with the statement "*in and through community lies the salvation of the world*". This insight is further reinforced by Albert Einstein, "*the individual if left alone from birth, would remain primitive and beastlike in thoughts and feelings to a degree that we can hardly conceive. The individual is what he is and has the significance that he has not so much in virtue of his individuality, but rather as a member of a great hu-*

man community, which directs his material and spiritual existence from the cradle to the grave."

The stories of community capacity building share several key features:

- believing in the capacity of people to share a common vision;
- inclusivity: everyone has a gift that can be included in the process of community;
- creating a process that celebrates the interconnectedness of everyone;
- creating and sustaining a shared decision-making process;
- awareness that the work of people is part of something larger than the sum of their individual parts;
- taking the time to care for the well being of one another;
- looking upon challenging circumstances as a way of celebrating capacities rather than identifying incapacities;
- sustaining a belief that community is not so much about institutions as it is about a process of building and sustaining healthy relationships;
- focusing on what can be done, not on what should be done;
- checking with everyone that the process is still aligned with the original vision;
- celebrate, with rituals, the gifts that everyone brings to the community building process;
- profound respect for self and others.

Ultimately, Community Capacity Building is about the nurturing and sustenance of healthy relationships. It is through building relationships that we find out who we are and what unique contributions we are able to bring to the world.

Independence..{is} middle-class blasphemy.
We are all dependent on one another, every soul of us on earth.
G.B. Shaw, Pygmalion, 1912

Community	Non-Community
Create ways to build relationship	Maintain blocks to relationships
Promote process of inclusion	Promote process of exclusion
Embrace conflict to address harm done	Encourage means to "fight" conflict
Experience feelings of safety	Experience feelings of fear
Feeling connected to others	Feeling fear of others and isolation
Promote ways to support, create development and growth of self and others	Promote ways that stifle growth and development of self and others
Attention to maintaining the well-being of the physical environment	Disregard and abuse of the physical environment

I've seen and met angels wearing the disguise
of ordinary people living ordinary lives.
Tracy Chapman

A society grows great when old men plant trees
whose shade they know they shall never sit in.
Greek proverb

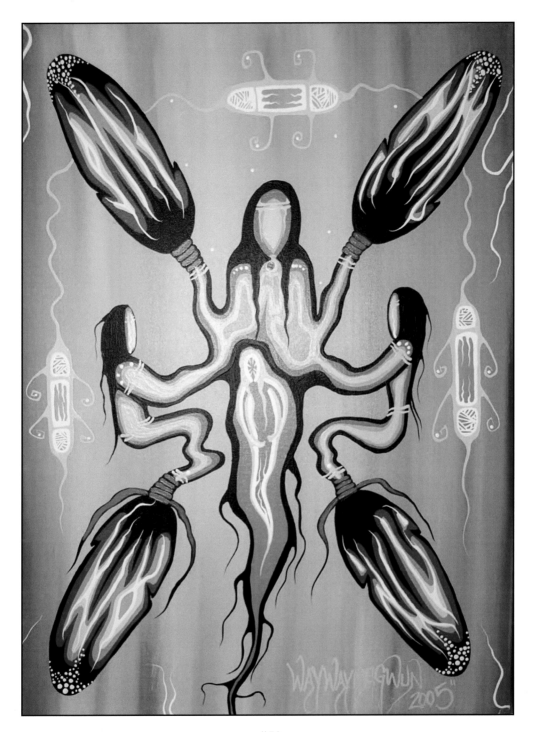

#59
"A Child Within"

It is within, where the child lies. Around us there are directions to seek out, but within us there lives a child that works when there is work to do, and he knows how to play when he is at work creating that mystical energy, which sustains us all.

Creating Community Partnerships

In recent years the media has greatly increased its coverage and commentary on the issues of youth crime. Rarely a day passes without news items on youth violence in our schools and communities. This has created a heightened awareness (albeit somewhat distorted) of the state of affairs in our schools. The media coverage has brought the issues to the forefront and has allowed us an opportunity to test our beliefs concerning crime and punishment.

Those who adhere to the " nail 'em and jail 'em " approach call for stricter rules and tougher punishments. These proponents are satisfied with zero tolerance... removing offending students from the classroom. However, there are long-range consequences connected with removing youth from school and forcing them into the community... especially the societal costs associated with creating a "casualty class" of youth who no longer have access to education, who are unprepared for employment, who lack the skills necessary to be contributing members of their community. When we disenfranchise youth from school communities we merely move the problems and the increased expense to another arena, whether it be the justice system or social services.

Taking a restorative approach to the issues of school violence allows us an opportunity to reflect on what needs to be done. The focus is no longer on the rules that have been broken and the punishment that should follow, but rather on the relationships that have been damaged, the harm caused to the community, and the ways in which things can be made right again... and avoided from happening in the future.

Creating community partnerships is never easy. There are territorial and mandate issues, funding sources, and manpower considerations. Often there are hundreds of reasons why we cannot work together, and only one reason why we must. We cannot do it alone.

It has been our experience that when police, schools, courts, agencies and communities come together to tackle the problems of youth violence, the 'get tough' approach is rarely on the agenda, because the stance almost never produces a satisfying response to justice issues. Most often, stakeholders are looking for methods that will hold youth meaningfully accountable for their actions, will allow them an opportunity to make amends and will encourage reintegration back into the community... with the supports necessary for success.

Where to Begin:
Our Past

Examine the stakeholders in your community! Do the police divisions have separate units for youth crime and/or school liaison officers? Are there conflict mediation agencies? Have service organizations shown a willingness to help with youth initiatives? Does the school board have support staff or alternative programs which focus on safe schools issues?

The stakeholders' list will vary from community to community, but the goal is to start talking about big picture issues that involve everyone. Where does conflict occur? What kinds of harmful behaviours are occurring? What is the community's response? How could we do things differently?

When Restorative Justice training started at the Toronto District School Board, different areas of the Board targeted different issues. Two education offices set up processes through the local youth courts so that cases involving police charges could be referred (through the courts) for conferencing. Another education office targeted the under 12 population that could not be touched through the justice system. Yet a fourth office focused their attention on school related issues that were not serious enough to warrant police intervention. What was important was beginning a restorative process that would grow as needs were identified.

One major concern in any kind of new initiative is the funding and people resources necessary to get a project up and running. It has been our experience that creating a shared vision is the first step towards success. A Restorative Justice model does not necessarily mean creating a whole new program (with new funding sources), it may mean just doing our jobs differently. We now spend a great amount of resources, both staff and money, on a punishment model of justice. School boards have created whole areas devoted to safe schools issues. The justice system deals with ever increasing numbers through the courts and probation, and the police have units that deal exclusively with youth issues. These existing frameworks may be the best way to introduce a restorative approach... there need not be any additional costs if all the players agree to use a conferencing model as part of their service delivery.

School boards can offer conferencing as part of their safe schools initiatives. Conferencing can be included for bullying, truancy, and other issues that would be included in the student code of conduct... but also for cases involving suspensions and expulsions. Where police are involved, conferencing can occur as part of a caution or may be included along with charges being laid. Courts are able to recommend conferencing as part of an alternative measure, or for more serious cases, when all parties agree that the process would be useful.

Restorative practices can be used along the justice continuum at any stage, if it is felt that the process would have better results than the current punishment models. Conferencing is time consuming but research shows that those who commit offending behaviour are far less likely to re-offend after going through the circle experience. Therefore, rather than processing the same youth time and again, either through suspensions or court, it would become a cost saving measure to do things once... with lasting results.

Where to Begin: Our Present

The Youth Criminal Justice Act calls upon communities and families to work in partnership in order to address the underlying causes of youth crime. The act emphasizes the need to rehabilitate and reintegrate young persons into society, taking into account their maturity level and the importance of timely interventions and meaningful consequences. It speaks to the need to provide guidance and support and that interventions should reinforce respect for societal values, encourage the repair of harm done and take into consideration the needs of the victim. It seems self evident that our Safe Schools policies and procedures should be guided by these same principals of rehabilitation and reintegration. Our schools play a key role in the development of good citizenship, moral development and community building.

Anti-Bullying Initiatives:

The issue of school bullying and victimization is of great concern in schools across Ontario. Research conducted in the spring of 2003 by the Canadian Public Health Association indicated that bullying has a profound impact on the victims.

The psychological damage that bullying can cause for student victims includes internalizing behavioural problems such as depression and social anxiety. Many otherwise well-adjusted students develop symptoms of internalizing problems following long-term exposure to bullying behaviour. At the very least, exposure to bullying behaviour at school is likely to exacerbate problems among students already pre-disposed to emotional difficulties. It is common for victims to experience low self-esteem, loneliness, and insecurity. A large proportion have difficulties making friends and maintaining social relationships. Many report blaming themselves and thinking that they are worthless. Depression and suicidal ideation can result, and suicide attempts (and in rare cases completions) have been found in many studies.

In David DeWit's study, approximately 45 percent of the 2,400 grade 9 students surveyed reported symptoms of physiological depression in the previous week (e.g., sluggishness, difficulty sleeping, poor appetite, and attention problems). Between 20 and 25 percent of all students reported frequently occurring symptoms of social anxiety. School engagement is directly affected; victims are likely to experience learning disruptions and refuse to attend school (due to fear of ongoing harm).   In this same study, about one in every three students reported that they did not feel included in school activities; ten percent did not feel accepted; and eighteen percent felt like they did not belong. Some studies have found that experiences of victimization at school are causally antecedent to the onset of mental health problems among children and adolescents.

In adulthood, victims are at elevated risk of suffering from low self-esteem, depression and other mental illnesses (such as schizophrenia and in rare cases suicide) and experiencing ongoing victimization in interpersonal relationships. Overall, victims tend to suffer more diverse problems compared to bullies. Given that anxiety and depression are not readily identifiable, victims also have a greater likelihood of suffering in silence. (1)Bullying, School Exclusion and Literacy Mark Totten and Perpetua Quigley

Canadian Public Health Association April 25, 2003,funded by Human Resources Development Canada National Literacy Secretariat.

In 2000 the Ontario government passed the Safe Schools Act that outlined the response schools should take when acts of violence occur. The Act focused on the exclusion of offenders by outlining behaviours that would warrant suspensions and expulsions but did little to meet the needs of the victims and the school communities harmed by the incident. Removal of the offenders often gave little comfort to the victims, it did nothing to resolve the underlying issues of violence/ bullying and often contributed to re-victimization when the offender returned to school.

The Restorative Justice process of Family Group Conferencing is designed to enhance interpersonal skills and develop empathy in students who are involved in school violence. The family group conferencing model brings together the offender, the victim, and their respective support people, as well as school staff and community members in order to process the nature of the offense, the harm that has been caused to all and ways in which that harm can be repaired. The model holds youth accountable for their actions in meaningful and direct ways. It addresses the needs of the victims and allows the school community to be part of the solution. It can also include the larger neighborhood in the process as often the violence present in our schools is carried over from issues outside the education context.

The Restorative Justice process has become an effective tool in dealing with school violence, bullying, gangs, truancy issues and other situations involving criminal charges. Teachers, school administrators, guidance counselors, social workers and police have used the family group conferencing model very successfully in school-related incidents. The conferencing model has direct application in suspension and expulsion policies as it relates to the mitigating factors that principals must consider. The model can be used effectively along a continuum of services from prevention to full expulsions.

This model provides some balance in a zero tolerance stance for school violence as it allows for those most directly involve to be part of a process that meets the needs of the victim and provides the offender with an opportunity to examine how their actions have harmed others. By listening to the victims directly, the offender can develop a sense of empathy and remorse and a willingness to right the wrong that has been done. The conferencing model also encourages community members to assist the youth in the rehabilitation process.

This model has been used successfully in policing and education in many countries throughout the world since the 1980's. It is currently being used by a number of school boards in Ontario as part of their Safe Schools initiatives. As of April 1st, 2003 conferencing is now a part of the Youth Criminal Justice Act and can be used at various points in the justice system including extrajudicial measures and extrajudicial sanctions. This addition to the youth justice system allows for greater flexibility in school violence issues as both police and school administrators search for ways to rehabilitate and reconnect youth.

The research points to some key features for creating safe schools including positive school culture, social skills development, discipline procedures that include victims, offenders and the larger school community, involvement of families, staff development and an ongoing plan for school improvement in the area of safe and caring schools. The Family Group Conferencing model allows schools to deal with bullying and victimization in a way which fosters community building and skill development. It provides the victim with a forum for expressing the impact the bullying has had on them. It also allows the victim to participate in solutions which will meet their personal needs. As families and community members are encouraged to be part of the circle process the conferencing format widens the safety net of adults involved and thus strengthens the supports offered to the victim. Conferencing also addresses the issue of the bystander problem by encouraging the peer group to participate in the circle. This gives some ownership of the problem to those who have watched the bullying without intervening on behalf of the victim. Conferencing encourages bystanders to take active measures to prevent future bullying by developing an action plan that is supported by all participants.

The school-based conferencing model will also meet the expectations of the Youth Criminal Justice Act by: reinforcing respect for societal values, encouraging the repair of harm done to victims and the community, treating victims with courtesy, compassion and respect and by giving victims the opportunity to participate and be heard. The conferencing model allows us to increase our support for victims of bullying and school violence as outlined in the board policies by giving school administrators a model which would be victim-centred, inclusive of all parties to the event and future-focused in terms of outcomes for all those effected.

Bullying - A Story

The social work department in our school board set a goal: learn about restorative justice as an alternative to traditional disciplinary measures used in schools (for a variety of interpersonal offences). Each of us came with a partner from our schools. We spent a very stimulating day with Arthur Lockhart, Randy Charboneau and Lynn Zammit.

The workshop was enriching and invigorating. The presenters shared their personal stories, and encouraged us to share some of our own. Defences were lowered, and very naturally, we were invited to immerse ourselves in the experience of community conferencing.

At the end of the day, many remarked what a fantastic experience it had been. Rather than feeling that all too familiar post-workshop heaviness and intellectual overload, we felt recharged and excited.

The feedback I have received following the community conferences I have facilitated in schools has been very positive. Participants, who were initially sceptical, have commented that circles have been the most helpful interventions they have been involved in. Previously, many had felt that problems were chronic and nothing could solve them.

Administrators told us that many traditional disciplinary approaches were like putting a Band-Aid on a gushing wound, and often made situations worse in the long run. By contrast, they felt that restorative justice was a "breath of fresh air" that provided an opportunity to help repair relationships between people.

Threats & Bullying:
An Elementary School Story

John Lanthier

The superintendent of education received a frantic telephone call from a grade 8 boy's father. A group of children had chased his son off the bus, all the way to his house. The children then stood outside the house yelling, while one member of the group argued with the boy's mother on the porch, threatening to beat the boy up. The father explained that his son had been chronically bullied for two years. He felt that past school interventions with the offenders had been ineffective in remedying the situation. In addition, his son had been suspended on a number of occasions, for what the father felt was self-defence.

Members of the Board's professional student support services were asked to intervene. On interviewing the children involved and their parents, it was discovered that the situation was far from a simple example of bullying. Many of the children had been both victims and perpetrators of bullying in the school and surrounding community. A system of mutual retaliation had been damaging relationships among these children for years. There had been several incidents with the original victim: being bullied on the bus; debris thrown into his backyard pool; rumours spread about him. This boy had also engaged in behaviours: spitting on other children's lunches; spreading rumours about others; punching others.

Younger siblings were also targeted as a means to get back at older combatants. In one case, a seven-year-old girl in grade two had been the victim of extortion. A boy in grade seven had successfully threatened her into paying him $5.00, which she had to steal from her own sister.

Older boys had been teaching younger boys how to bully others, including how to trip others. In so doing, a younger child had been hurt.

In addition, the parents of many of the children had engaged in arguments over their children's fights. Some of these arguments had become quite heated with parents yelling over their children's heads at each other. The adults felt that their counterparts were blind to their own children's behaviour and were not taking responsibility for the problems. The larger community was fractured.

With some education about restorative justice, the school administration agreed to allow us to organize a community conference. A significant amount of work was necessary to prepare the families, as most of their children had something 'act' for which they were responsibility.

The community conference was composed of five families, the school administration, and multiple facilitators, (Arthur Lockhart, Randy Charboneau and Lynn Zammit). We had 28 people sitting around the room. The meeting lasted close to three hours.

Rather than the traditional approach of having people in exclusive roles of offenders or victims and focussing on a specific incident, the children were all asked to speak about their experience of bullying in the school and surrounding community. Stories of different events were shared; some involved all of those present; others involved a portion of the group. Children talked about both their victimization, and their participation in bullying others. The parents talked about the impact these events had had on their children and their families. The parents of the initial victim discussed how they felt isolated in the community. They acknowledged that their son had retaliated against others.

The initial victim's mother was teary through most of the story sharing. She also described how her son had developed a nervous tick since the bullying had begun. She wept openly when a number of parents expressed empathy for what this boy and his family had been through.

Discussion ensued about what everyone needed to have happen to repair the harm. This was done in small groups, made possible with the large number of facilitators. The groups were divided to be heterogeneous by age and family membership. The ideas were then shared and agreements were made in the larger group.

Many of the agreements naturally evolved from a desire among these families to come together as a community. For instance, a number of the parents who were home in the mornings agreed to form a roster between them, so that they would share responsibility for greeting the children at the morning bus stop, and encourage the children to say good morning to each other.

The families agreed to meet on a monthly basis, and the school offered their gym for this purpose. These meetings would provide an opportunity for the parents to talk about how everyone was getting along. The group would be permitted to play with gym equipment, perhaps getting a game of indoor soccer going. One parent volunteered to coordinate the timing of the first meeting.

In addition, the principal offered to organize a regular recreational activity at school for the children involved in the circle.

Finally, some of the older boys in the circle expressed interest in changing the dynamic of their training of younger ones. It was agreed that the administration would arrange some education for these older boys, so that they could become positive mentors to those in younger grades regarding what to do about bullying.

Threats & Bullying
A High School Story
John Lanthier

A small town high school has been struggling with a chronic problem of bullying by a group of grade 10 girls. Almost all of the girls in grade 10 had, at one time or another, been victimized by the offenders.

The bullying was usually verbal, involving criticism of a person's attire or behaviour. The victim was called degrading, derogatory names. Rumours were spread about the victim. Being a small school, by the end of the day, many youths approached victims to ask if the rumours were true.

When witnesses saw the targeting begin, they did not support their friends to stop the bullying. Since they had all been victimized, they did nothing, because they were relieved it was not their turn that day. Those that defended a friend were bullied even worse. Threats of physical harm were also used to intimidate would be allies.

The result was that the victim ended up feeling totally isolated.

Due to fear of physical retribution, and the 'code' that says, "Thou shall not be a rat," the victims were very hesitant to report the abuse.

A group of these victims agreed to come together in a bystander's support group. This group had been meeting to discuss ways to support one another in the face of this rampant bullying.

In the meantime, one of the bullies had a falling out with her friends. As is the nature with this group, loyalties are very fragile. This girl began to experience very intense bullying, both at school and via MSN and websites. Threats of physical harm were made. This girl expressed interest in becoming part of the support group.

Initially, the existing support group refused, as almost everyone had been bullied by this girl. However, they agreed, as did the bully, to participate in a healing circle to see if relationships could be repaired.

The circle was attended by the bully, one support person who was already a member of the support group (but had not been directly bullied by this particular offender), seven victims, two facilitators and the school vice principal. The offender took responsibility for her past behaviour towards the group, and then listened as each victim told the story of how she had been affected. Parents were not involved in this circle, but the victims spoke of how the bullying at school had affected their relationships with their families. They shared feelings of anxiety, terror and depression.

Several of the victims spoke through tears. The offender cried through most of the meeting, and made a very sincere apology to everyone.

To begin to repair the harm, many of the girls were just looking for that apology. Some revealed that mistrust was still present. However, they acknowledged that the victim's agreement to participate in the circle and listen to their experiences without becoming defensive went a long way to repair that mistrust.

In addition to reaching an agreement that the offender would maintain a respectful relationship with everyone in the circle, the group unanimously agreed to accept the offender into their ongoing support group meetings.

Conferencing Methodology:

INFORMATION FOR PARTICIPANTS

What is a Family Group Conference:

A Family Group Conference is a meeting of community people who have been affected by behaviour that has caused serious harm. The conference provides a forum in which the parties to an incident can come together to examine the factors that led to the harmful actions, the impact that behaviour has had on the lives of others and possible ways in which order can be restored to that community. The circle process allows all parties to be part of a consensus approach and encourages all significant interests to be represented and respected. It allows a voice to all those who have been harmed and participation in the decisions concerning what should be done to repair the harm. The conferencing format creates a safe, problem-solving environment that can significantly reduce further harm:

> • by addressing the underlying causes of crime;
> • by encouraging the participants to rebuild a sense of community;
> • by reconnecting people in trouble with the supports necessary for future

success. Those who have given offense are held meaningfully accountable for their behaviour, in ways that encourage reintegration back into the community.

Who Attends a Conference:

A conference usually involves:

> • those who caused the harm and their supporters;
> • those who were harmed by the incident and their supporters;
> • the conference facilitator (who is formally trained and experienced)
> • anyone else from the community who has a role to play in the event (school administration, police where there has been charges laid)

The Conferencing Process

When an incident is referred for a Restorative Justice conference a trained facilitator is assigned to the case. This person will investigate the incident and determine if a conference should be held. There are a number of conditions that must be met before a conference can proceed:

   • those who caused the harm must admit guilt;
   • those who caused the harm must demonstrate a sense of remorse:
   • those who caused the harm must be willing to make amends to their victim(s).

If these conditions are satisfied then the facilitator will contact those who have been harmed in order to invite them to join the process. If the two parties are willing to proceed, then the facilitator contacts the school administration for their consent and, in cases involving police charges, the officer in charge of the case is asked to approve the process. In some cases approval through the courts may be necessary. If there is consensus that a conference should take place, all parties are notified and a date is set. The facilitator will contact all the circle participants prior to that date, and in many cases will meet with them privately in order to gain a better understanding of the events, to discuss the circle process, and answer any questions they may have.

The Circle Experience

All participants involved in the circle are given an opportunity to recount their view of what happened at the time of the harmful event, and how their lives have been affected by the incident. The damage is often emotional as well as physical. It is important that everyone have a clear understanding of the full impact of the behaviour. They then decide what needs to be done to repair the damage and minimize further harm. When an agreement has been reached it is written up in the form of a contract that all participants sign. The contract usually contains time lines for any kind of restitution. Copies of the contract are given to each person, and in the case of incidents involving police charges, a copy is sent back to court for the next appearance date. It is important to note that the outcomes of a conference have no legal bearing on the outcomes of a court decision. It is up to the courts to decide how the contract agreement will be taken into consideration. The facilitator will do a follow up at a later date to determine that all parts of the contract have been completed.

Conferencing Methodology:

PRE-CIRCLE

An event has taken place that results in your being asked to facilitate a restorative justice circle. The following elements must be addressed for the building of a successful circle.

- **collect information from the people** who have already gathered the information   (i.e. vice-principal, police, guidance):

- **meet with the persons** most directly involved in the event:
   a) the person who engaged in the offending behavior;
   b) the person who was victimized by the offending behavior;
   c) supporters of the person who engaged in the offending behavior;
   d) supporters of the person who was victimized by the offending behavior;

- in meeting with the people it is important to **be clear about what the circle is about:**
   a) an opportunity to create ways to help repair the harm that has been done;
   b) an opportunity for the person who has been victimized by the event to have a voice in what could be done to help repair the harm;
   c) an opportunity for the person who engaged in the offending behavior to   demonstrate that they have the capacity and the responsibility to help repair the harm that has been done;
   d) an opportunity for the person who was victimized by the event to realize they have the support of members of the community in this process
   e) an opportunity for the person who committed the offending behavior to see the impact they have had on people
   f) an opportunity to demonstrate that a process guided by principles of respect and community is a powerful and meaningful way of addressing the events that created harm

It is crucial to be clear that you are not representing the offender or the victim.
Your role is to facilitate a process that has as its primary goal the opportunity to create ways to help repair the harm that has taken place. It is important that the participants

are aware of your formal role within the organization where you work.

It is important to meet in person with as many of the circle participants as possible, prior to the actual circle. In the event you are able to meet only over the phone, ensure that you will have some time with them even if it is only 10 minutes prior to the circle. Your presence will be the common thread that holds the circle together.

Do not offer guarantees about what will happen in terms of outcomes i.e. "the offender will probably get a lengthy suspension, all criminal charges will be dropped". The only certainty that you can speak to is that you are here to facilitate a process that is based on principles of respect, community, creativity and the opportunity to mutually assess steps that will help repair the harm.

Once it is determined that you will in fact be facilitating the circle and you have the participants determined, it is important to arrange for the site where the circle will take place.

Restorative Justice:

A Reflection

Angel Yuen

"When I was initially approached about facilitating a Restorative Justice Circle with 7 offenders involved in shoplifting, I was intrigued and curious. I had gone to a 3 day Restorative Justice training with Lynn Zammit and Art Lockhart, but had not yet facilitated a circle, and was excited about the first opportunity. As I had more time to think about what it meant, I had many worries about whether or not it would be feasible, especially involving 18 participants. After consulting with Restorative Justice Facilitators, I was encouraged to go ahead and rely on each person's capacities to 'make it happen'.

The planning was three and a half weeks of preparation. There were several interviews, phone calls and consultations. There was also the unfolding of people's reactions, emotions, and sometimes fear of coming together in such a large circle group.

Once I started co-ordinating, I too became involved in a way I would not have imagined. In the preparation meetings there was often anger, sadness, disappointment and tears. All participants were clearly affected by the events. I was struck by the sadness there was for parents, and how it seemed that many had never felt a sense of belonging in their community. Some parents had lost faith in the school system. Almost all the parents of the offending behavior kids wanted to keep their child away from their peers. One mother even talked of planning to move to another city, while another mother had quit her job as a result of the events. This made bringing the Circle together even more important as it would help build a sense of community.

The co-ordination became overwhelming at times. There were moments of high stress in dealing with the many pieces. There were issues of language, learning disability, time restraints, non-accountability, blame and isolation.

Nevertheless, throughout the process of planning and preparation, I always kept in mind that 'everyone' had the capacity to 'make it happen' and that the Circle was about 'shared responsibility.' It was during these moments that Art helped ground me and provide me with reassurance. The anchor for any Circle is the relationships and this helped me to 'let go' of some of the issues. It allowed me to listen and understand people's fears and worries.

The Circle meeting was 2 hours and 20 minutes. Some parents were ambivalent and anxious, and it was these parents who were quite expressive during the Circle.

There was a feeling of connectedness (rather than blame... which they worried about) as each was able to share their voice and reach a common ground. Each parent had worries for their children, which were similar to the next parent. The parents together provided creative, enthusiastic and realistic ideas and ways to repair the harm. More important, all made authentic apologies to a store manager who was harmed in their community. He talked of his experience of being affected... not only as a store manager but also as a father and a wage earner. The Circle took away the annonymity of the shoplifting and showed the personal harm.

Each of the kids who offended showed courage by taking responsibility and owning up to the harm they had caused. After the Circle they said that it would now be possible to say "Hi" to the vice-principal again, and smile at him in the school hallway. Prior to the Circle they had been feeling like the "bad kids" of the school.

After the Circle many participants stayed behind to say "Thank You".

Three months later...

I had the opportunity to facilitate a second circle and most Restorative Justice facilitators would probably agree that the second circle was easier (and calmer). 'Self Surveillance' was not overtaking me since I had the experience of knowing, believing, and trusting the Circle to repair the harm in a meaningful way. Now I could truly rely on the first circle experience to take me through the process with more confidence.

The experience of being involved in Restorative Justice Circles has touched my professional life in a profound way. As a social worker, it has provided me with meaningful work, in ways which go well beyond the therapy room.

One final side bar, one of the original offending students contributed an article about peer pressure and shoplifting, which was included in a student-developed pamphlet on Peer Pressure."

Conferencing Goals

• to educate our youth as to the impact their actions have had on others;

• to encourage the capacity of the individual to create actions in a meaningful and constructive way;

• to provide people with a means to make amends to their victim(s);

• to provide an opportunity for the persons victimized to have their voices heard, while arriving at ways to repair the harm.

Few things help an individual more
than to place responsibility upon him,
and to let him know that you trust him.
Booker T. Washington

Conference Objectives

• to help keep youth connected to their schools and communities;

• to decrease the disruption to the educational programs of offenders and victims;

• to maintain a safe learning environment in our schools;

• to provide community-based alternatives to the court system;

• to address the root causes of violence and to repair harm;

• to offer the victim and the offender support and resolution;

• to provide at-risk youth with appropriate community programs and services;

• to foster interracial and ethnocultural harmony and cooperation;

• to strengthen home, school, police and community partnerships;

• to assist communities in finding solutions to key community safety issues;

• to reduce the financial, emotional and quality of life costs of crime.

A great many people think they are thinking when
they are merely rearranging their prejudices.
William James

Conference
Outcomes

• people are held meaningfully accountable for their behaviour;

• victims are given a strong voice in the justice process;

• the matter is dealt with in a time frame that initiates closure and encourages healing for everyone involved;

• it is more financially cost effective than any other form of intervention;

• the community has a key part to play in the conferencing process.

Cowardice asks the question - is it safe? Expediency asks the question - is it politic? Vanity asks the question - is it popular? But conscience asks the question - is it right? And there comes a time when one must take a position that is neither safe, nor politic, nor popular; but one must take it because it is right.
Dr. Martin Luther King, Jr.

Conferencing Methodology:

ENVIRONMENT of the MEETING PLACE

- The site will likely be held in a school, and usually after school hours.

- The room must be one that will not have outside interruptions, i.e. beware of using someone else's office (School libraries tend to be conducive for this type of meeting).

- Ensure that the school intercom system will not interfere with the meeting.

- Ensure that there are refreshments such as juice, coffee, finger foods.

- Ensure that all cell phones have been turned off.

- Ensure that there is no phone in the room, or have it disconnected.

- Ensure that any participants have not left messages where they can be contacted.

- Ensure that enough time has been allotted for the facilitation of the circle. While each circle is unique allotting 3 hours tends to allow more than enough time.

- Ensure that people know who will be participating in the circle.

In your pre-meeting with the participants you will have gone over the questions that you will be focusing on in the circle.

- Ensure that you will be the only one taking notes, and that the purpose of the note is to summarize the agreed to outcomes

- Ensure the seating arrangement is in a circle. The circle flows, for example, with the facilitator at the center/top of the circle, continuing from the left, the offender, followed by the closest supporters of the offender, continuing around with other members who have been affected by the event, completing the circle with the supporters of the victim and the victim on the right hand side of the facilitator.

- Ensure that everyone can see and hear everyone else, that no one is given a seat that is higher or different than everyone else.

- In the instance where small children need to be accommodated, ensure that there is someone who could be in the role of 'sitter' and that a room is available for the children

- Have a box of Kleenex on hand, circles can be emotive.

#60
"Between Them"

The feather is the symbol of endurance, curiosity, path, flight. As a couple they work at defining these words, feelings. Together they know love and life. Together they walk.

Conferencing Methodology:

ROLE OF THE FACILITATOR

There is a wonderful Zen saying:
"the art of Zen is doing nothing, but doing nothing very well."

This quote can be applied to the facilitator in the restorative justice circle. Up to the point of bringing everyone to the circle, the facilitator's role has been to guide, support, clarify, and set the context of safety for the meeting. By this stage, all the participants of the circle will have an appreciation for the idea of '*taking steps to repair the harm*'. In the event that negativity was to surface during the circle, this is the phrase that is best used as a form of anchor. To illustrate: a participant is displaying anger, and is talking over others to the point of distracting from the purpose of the meeting. This is the time where the facilitator can say: "when we met previously we agreed that the purpose of coming here today was to explore ways to repair the harm." This statement is often powerfully supported by the use of a justice symbol such as a talking stone or talking stick. The benefits of this symbol include: equity - while the person is holding the talking stone, everyone is affording him/her respect through listening.

Following the principle of "*do nothing but do it very well*" here are some additional principles that have proven to guide the circle in a healthy way:

Listening Vs Waiting to Speak: Waiting to speak is an element pervasive in the criminal court process. In fact the rule of operation is to never ask a question for which you do not know the answer. The outcome of this practice can often be an insincere experience. Listening, true listening invites people to feel their voice will be heard. Listening in this format is not framed in an inquisitorial fashion. Rather, listening simply but effectively, invites people to hear, perhaps for the first time, the truth of the issue is in terms of what transpired.

Authenticity: Simply being yourself is perhaps one of the single most important gifts that you bring to the role of facilitation. It is crucial that the participants of the circle see you as a person who is genuinely attending to the principle of helping to repair the harm that has taken place. Focusing on this goal allows participants to feel safe in sharing.

Humour: There is a great difference between joke telling (did you hear the one about…) and creative humour. Humour in this context is about the capacity to release tension that may be hindering the process. Humour does not minimize the experience, rather it creates a context for creativity and compassion.

Intelligence and Wisdom: There is a Taoist saying: "to achieve intelligence add something everyday, to achieve wisdom remove something everyday". As a facilitator one of the greatest challenges is to engage the role of facilitator, not the role of counselor, therapist, mediator, social worker, investigator or adjudicator. The purpose of the circle is to allow the creativity, capacity, and experience of the community participants to be the focal points... not the facilitator. The role is to set the atmosphere that allows everyone's ideas and feelings to be heard and respected. The participants, and not the facilitator, will come up with outcomes and action steps, and accountability for what must now take place.

There will be many times throughout the course of the circle that you will feel that you could frame things in a way that 'is right for everyone' (what I hear you saying is…). This is when you are to do nothing very well. Trust the process to let the participants creatively pursue the outcomes they feel are key. In essence, the script (set questions) best guides the circle. In some cases, a facilitator may assist someone struggling with a question (e.g. "whom have you seen affected by this event?" Answer: no response followed by "I don't know"... the facilitator may follow with "if there was someone in the group here who was affected who do you think it might be, how do you think they might have been affected by what happened?")

By beginning the question with the word "if", you are making it safe for the person to come up with an answer. The "if" question does not hold the immobilization that comes when someone is told "well you <u>should</u> know."

Silence: Allowing for people to listen, truly listen is reinforced through periods of silence. Often our collective experience has been to fill up silence with something- words, sounds, in the circle. Giving pause after someone has spoken is a demonstration of respect for what they have just shared. This is critical, especially if you feel the urge to move on to the next person right away. Silence has the effect of bringing a sense of calm to the process. Silence allows for reflection (and, hopefully, wisdom to guide the discussion).

Symbols: Having the space to share one's voice is essential in any healing process. The function of symbols such as talking sticks, talking stones, and feathers, have been in use for centuries. The strength of having some form of symbol is found in providing the opportunity for one to feel that this is his or her time to be heard, and everyone will be listening. It may also limit people from taking over one another. This symbol creates a sense of equity. Regardless of one's role, everyone has their time to express their feelings, no one is more important than the other. Everyone talks through the security of the symbol.

Some facilitators use the symbol only at the beginning of the circle as a form of introduction, and at the completion of the circle as part of the closure.

Some facilitators prefer not to use the symbol at all. They feel it takes away the spontaneity of possible key elements of group dynamics.

Acknowledgement: Thanking people for coming to the circle at the outset of the process is fundamental to getting off on the "right foot". Unlike the court system where people are called forward and put on the 'witness stand', here you indicate at the outset that a first, healthy step is being taken just by being here. For many people just the act of showing up has taken a great deal of courage.

Restorative Justice
at Oolagen Community Services

Faye Forde

Over a year ago, Oolagen Community Services, my employers, presented the idea of training in the area of restorative justice. I had heard of the process, and understood it to man a process in which the person responsible for the offending behaviour sits with the victim of the offence, as well as others impacted by the incident. I had grave concern that this would create more harm for the victim.

At the training, we heard stories from presenters and co-workers. I began to feel that the restorative justice process might be an opportunity to do something different and creative in addressing offensive behaviour. In my work setting, when a youth committed an offence, the result was usually discharge from the program. This was discouraging to both the youth and the team. After the training, I felt excited, charged with new of hope to assist youth in processing their actions and behaviour.

Months later, I had the opportunity to put the training to the test. Our circle came about after a young lady, who struggles with a very explosive temper, assaulted a team staff member. This was particularly difficult, as the staff member was her primary worker, and had built a strong relationship with this young woman. It was difficult for the staff to entertain the idea of charging the youth, let alone having her removed from our program.

I suggested that we did not have to lose her. Instead, we could propose doing a circle with all those involved. We could also proceed with the charge. Everyone involved in the incident liked the idea, so a circle was planned. The offending youth, her CAS {SPELL IT OUT} worker, 2 staff members, and 2 youths who witnessed the violence, all agreed to participate.

As the facilitator, I was excited about the impending opportunity for all to have their voices heard. At the same time, I was ambivalent, worrying whether this would go well. This young woman had genuine difficulty seeing/hearing how others were impacted and felt about her behaviour. I was also concerned for another youth who expressed some fear about speaking out about his peer and how she makes him feel. In the pre-interviews, it was clear how much the incident and the fear had impacted this young man. I was sad and angry that anyone should have to live feeling fear in the place they reside.

The circle went very well. I felt joy and sadness when the offender spoke of how she did not want people to fear her, and how she did not realize the impact of her actions on so many others. At the end of the circle, the offender's worker (CAS) expressed gratitude for being a part of this process. She had been unfamiliar with Restorative Justice, and was grateful for the opportunity to learn about it.

The youth, who had been fearful of sharing, said he felt positive about the experience. He hoped this could be a new beginning where he could feel safe in his placement. The victim, our staff member, was satisfied, and was also happy with the offender's acknowledgement. It was her belief and hope that this would be a new start with the young woman.

The outcome was that the offender, this young woman who had been with our program for 6 months, acknowledged that she needed help to manage her anger. She agreed to start a 5-week anger management group for girls, as well as resume 1:1 counselling. She also stated that she did not want anyone to fear her again.

The experience of doing the restorative justice circle has left its mark on us. It has influenced our work, and given us an alternative meaningful way to deal with offending behaviours in the future.

Weapons:
Stories from a Group Home
for at-risk Youth

Karen Jackson

Working in a group home residence presents many challenges. For example, how do you respond to behavior that may be classed a "dangerous" or "risky" to the other clients and staff? In the residence where I work, we were recently trained in a new way of thinking. It opened up integration of alternative intervention possibilities when dangerous situations occur in settings like our group home.

We received Restorative Justice Training and were trained in facilitating circles. We were taught about the importance of Pausing and inviting all people involved in an event to discuss how they came to be involved in the situation. We learned important questions:
- What were you thinking?
- What were you feeling?
- What has your experience been since the events took place?
- Whom have you seen affected by this event?

The story began when staff members found illegal drugs in one of the bathrooms in our group home. None of the young people who were present took responsibility for bringing the substances into the group home. This precipitated a house wide search. We needed to complete a full house search to ensure that there were no other such substances on property. During the search, staff found a switchblade in the possession of one of the youth. He acknowledged that it was his switchblade.

We did not suspect him of carrying the weapon, and we were very shocked to find it in his possession. The team was very conflicted on how to respond. Half of the team wanted to have him discharged or suspended. The other half felt that he was not aware of the seriousness of the offence and that he should be given a warning. Traditionally, this type of situation would result in a police intervention, possibly a suspension, or even discharge.

One thing the team agreed on was that to respond immediately would have been an injustice to the young person. Clearly the team was struggling with its own feelings and possibly reacting with individual beliefs and thoughts. The team felt that the best response would be no response - at least until we had put some thought into it. After much thinking, we PAUSED.

The young man made a commitment to keep the house safe until we could come up with the appropriate follow up or consequence.

We felt that this was a great chance to practice Restorative Justice. The young man agreed to participate in the process to repair the harm. We invited his parents as supports for him. They talked about being hopeful that he was willing to participate in the process. They were glad that the violation of safety did not result in more police involvement. They also talked about wanting to talk to him later about why he felt that he needed to have a weapon. Was it for protection? The staff members who worked that night were also part of the circle. They talked about feeling that they did not keep the house safe, and that the young person was at risk to harm himself, somebody in the home, or someone in the community.

The young man had the chance to hear all these concerns in a way that made it non-threatening to accept responsibility for his actions. He heard how other people were affected. He signed a contract and agreed to all the recommendations that were made.

That was a magical moment. Does that happen all the time? I am not sure. This was the only circle that I was part of. I would like to do more. As a rule, we find that young people that we work with are reluctant to take this step. Repairing harm is not something a 16yr old typically thinks about. However, I can say that we have had other magic moments, linked to the philosophy and practice of restorative justice as it becomes more and more a part of the culture of our group home.

• A young person stole from a staff member's purse, then came to staff several months later wanting to talk about what they had done and wanted "to repair the harm."

• A physical altercation occurred. The young people involved talked about how they were affected, who else they saw affected, and what they needed to happen to repair the harm. They even created their own signed and witnessed contract.

In our experience, the training has allowed us to be creative in how we respond to situations. Yet, there are times when we still ask clients to leave the program for violating safety. We still have a ways to go. But somehow it feels different in this house in this evolving role that we play in their lives in this ever-challenging work we do.

#62
"Across from me"

Outside this sacred lodge, a being offers a prayer to the Creator. Within the lodge he looks across and observes the Great Eagle of the Eastern Direction. He raises his feather and acknowledges the eagle. The eastern direction is where life begins and knowledge is formed.

Five Key Elements of Transformation

Within The Philosophy of Restorative Justice

A great many people think they are changing
when they are just rearranging their prejudices.
William James, Philosopher

Why must anyone seek for new ways of acting?
The answer is that in the long run the continuity
of life itself depends on the making of new (paradigms)...
The continuous invention of new ways of seeing
(and being) is (our) special secret of living.
J.Z.Young, Biologist

Deep in the core of all that is emerging about restorative justice in its many manifestations is transformation. Transformation is driving restorative justice up into the consciousness of society. While there are many wonderful outcomes from the efforts of those involved in bringing restorative justice into the life of society, it is vital that restorative justice not mutate into just another fleeting program. When pushed beyond the margins of justice practices, the pure elements of transformation in restorative justice may be lost. That is why they must be explored.

Transformation relates to Restorative Justice through Five Key Elements

The first element is Community
The greatest security we can have is a healthy community. The essence of community is brought to life by relationships. Relationships bring meaning into our lives. Relationships provide us with identity, purpose, meaning, direction. In essence, relationship, and therefore community is a life-giving, life-defining, life-nurturing process. Community is the interconnectedness of everything. No living organism within the universe survives without relating to the Other. We are in a relationship with everyone: our family, our friends, our colleagues, our neighborhood, town, city, country, and planet. Understanding the essence of community immediately introduces us to the exploration of relationships and their meaning for humanity. When we speak about a person who has come into conflict in life, it is impossible to talk about them without referring to the

absence of healthy life-affirming relationships. Conflict on the social level is about the denigration, the deterioration, and ultimately the neglect of relationships. Neglect of relationships is very often a product of retributive justice. (Retributive Justice is our current 'justice philosophy' which assigns punishments that are considered to be morally right and fully deserved.)

Retributive justice first and foremost is an oxymoron. Retribution does not, and will not create justice. Rather retributive justice increases the devolution and disintegration of community. Retributive justice focuses on assessing blame to individuals. Once achieved, the process then characterizes guilt to exact punishment. Punishment often highlights an individual's flaws and deficiencies, characterized by language such as "bad", "mean", "offender". These labels tend to define the entire person. In essence, we stigmatize in order to make the person stop committing offences.

Finally, retributive justice segregates from community by its explicit efforts to isolate and remove the "guilty" person from that community. Sadly this isolation/incarceration tends to have the reverse impact on addressing crime: the greater the amount of incarceration, the greater the likelihood of the person re-offending

Prof. Anthony Doob (University of Toronto) conducted a study that concluded that youth receiving a custody sentence were 7 times more likely to re-offend than those who did not. Additionally, the Canadian Federal Department of Justice stated: "incarceration was overused... Sentencing decisions resulted in unfairness in youth sentencing... YOA did not ensure effective reintegration of a young person after being released from custody."

For further reading see: http://canada.justice.gv.ca - then go to YCJA EXPLAINED. This site makes explicit reference to the over-use of custody and failure at reintegration.

Community at its zenith is about integration, not isolation. It is about celebrating capacities, not admonishing weakness. Community is about seeking creative compassionate ways to relate with one another, flaws, strengths, and all.

The opportunity in restorative justice is to constantly ask and demonstrate ways to create meaningful relationships and community, particularly in times of conflict and crisis.

The second element is Capacity

The Capacity of any human being is never created or nurtured in isolation. Capacity is created in and through relationships of one being with another. Capacity has many powerful opportunities to challenge anyone authentically engaging the process of restorative justice.

> • let go of favourite ways of thinking.

> • do not be prescriptive in the attempt to resolve the issue one is dealing with.

> • invite others into the circle of capacity building.

The invitation of others into a restorative justice process must be understood as an invitation for people to contribute their gifts, talents, insights and abilities in ways that can bring about or support the well-being of all involved in the process. When people are invited to participate in this way, true meaningful action and accountability is created.

The strength that is created here comes from everyone mutually developing the process and the outcomes, rather than having the outcomes imposed by a higher authority. This is a strength-based element rather than a deficiency-based element. If the goal is sustaining healthy community, then one key is to encourage the capacity of everyone to flourish, especially in times of conflict. In the event of a person hurting another person, the goal is not to hurt the person back. Rather, the pursuit is to explore how we draw on each other's capacities to help repair the harm that has been done. When capacity is explored, there are some immediate outcomes. People are not alienated and isolated, rather they are drawn together to repair harm.

Peoples' creativity is explored with the statements of 'We can...' or, 'I am able and willing to...' People, whether the person who committed the offending behavior, or the one who has been victimized, now have the opportunity to demonstrate strengths rather than shrink under shadows of retributive shame through a myopic focus framed within labeled limitations. Limitations are generated through the imposition of Shoulds.

Shoulds are the antithesis of capacity. When one is told what they should do, the effect is to deplete energy. The imposition of shoulds has the affect of "shoulding all over the person". The outcomes of "shouldings" are feelings of: anxiety, incapacity, despair, guilt, low self-esteem.

The outcomes of exploring capacity are the enhanced experience of ability, energy, and self-worth. When we focus on capacity, everyone is invited to contribute to the reparation of the harm that has been done. When capacity is explored, new and healthy relationships are formed. Remember: nothing meaningful is ever created in isolation. Capacity is realized in the circle process. People connect with and to their emotional, cognitive and spiritual levels and see these elements in relation to everyone else within the circle.

The third element is Connection

Disconnection is without doubt the purest manifestation of people in conflict. The Hopi Indians of North America have a word Koyaanisqatsi which translates: 'crazy life, life in turmoil, life disintegrating, life out of balance, a state of life that calls for another way of living'. I suggest that Koyaanisqatsi could be applied to our planet as a whole in present day experience. Just look around; tell me what you see. Retribution is aligned with "life disintegrating."

People who harm others often are disconnected from empathy for others. Often, they do not see themselves as having had a significant impact in the lives of others. Often they are instructed (within the criminal justice system) not to contact people affected by their behaviour and not to demonstrate empathy to the people affected by their behaviour.

Disconnection is also the manifestation of competition. Within the existing criminal justice system, the operating paradigm is disconnection through competition. The criminal justice system is often acting out the play: Us Against Them. Furthermore, it is not unusual for the person who was victimized to be excluded in cases involving a plea bargain. The result is no closure for the trauma they have experienced. Still deeper, when people who have been victimized sit through a full trial, they often come away feeling no true answer to why they were victimized. The disposition (retribution sentencing) does little to deal with the trauma they experience.

Connection, on the other hand, offers us the opportunity to explore and integrate "another way of living." Through connecting in a circle process, there is a fundamental shift from "I" to "We." In the circle process, people connect/reconnect with:
• their comprehension of the impact of their behaviour on others,
• their capacity to empathize with others,
• their ability to create ways - collaboratively - to repair the harm that has taken place,
• the truth of what transpired (the offending behaviour), rather than competing for the proof of what transpired.

There comes a point in the circle process, the "ah ha" moment, when participants realize that everyone is connected to everyone else. People are not isolated from one another. Through the circle process, they move into a transformative connection, because everyone does matter. That "ah ha" moment can only take place when everyone listens to everyone else.

The fourth element is Voice

"There is a world of difference between waiting to speak and listening." The significance of voice in the circle process cannot be overstated. Voice has two immediate compelling outcomes: 1) People are allowed to express the truth of their experience, and 2) Everyone listens to the person speaking. Often the most powerful outcome of a circle is the simple experience of being listened to for the very first time. When a person feels heard, truly heard, they also experience acknowledgement.

A person's experience is validated by having others hear and therefore feel their story. It takes great courage to tell a story where you have harmed others, and you want to acknowledge the pain you have caused. One person who had caused others great pain stated: "You learn on a very deep, emotional level the impact you have had when you hear the voice of each person in that circle. By the time everyone has spoken, you arrive at a place that is much deeper than you would have ever thought possible. There is a voice that comes from within when you are trying to say you are sorry, not from the surface, but from way deep down within yourself."

Equally, it takes great courage to move past a state of being victimized, to a place where you can tell others of your experience, and to see that you are not limited by the label of 'victim'. You can be a person with a strong, powerful voice; a voice that is heard by others, and felt by others. "As well as being an offender (robberies, aggravated assault, assault with weapons), I have also been a victim (child sexual abuse, neglect).

The greatest feeling I can have is letting go of the hate, anger and pain I feel towards those who harmed me. Now I am able to let all that go, because I was able to say out loud, 'Listen, I am hurting, and I have been carrying it for so long (this pain and anguish), it no longer belongs to me. I am letting it go.'"

Another person, who had also suffered sexual abuse as a child, had this to say about voice:

"Somehow, at times it feels like our culture has encouraged us not to speak and say out loud that we have been hurt, so we push the pain inside ourselves. And the deeper we push, the harder we push, the more painful the entire experience becomes. Then we create unhealthy self-destructive ways to block the pain, such as fighting, alcoholism, drug addiction. Just so my pain would not be noticeable to me, I would drink to the point of alcohol poisoning. I would self-sabotage as soon as I got close to achieving success. The reason I engaged in di-ssociative, self-harming behaviour was I would be snap back there, 'bang', that as a 12 year old boy, I had messed up. The man who sexually abused me was in his 30'. But somehow, it was all my fault, therefore I don't deserve good things. And the most debilitating aspect of all this was my loss of voice. I felt that I could not tell anyone about the horror that had happened. I believed if I did, I would be seen as someone who was weak, someone who brought it on himself. No matter how you framed, I was in the wrong. Over the years, my loss of voice was more and more muted by behaviour that was excessive: drinking to excess, fighting, drugs to excess, everything was done in excess. All this because my pain was 'in excess'.

When I look back on this story now, I think to myself. If I could have had a sense of safety where I could say that I was hurt; if somebody had listened to me, without judging me; if someone had just let me talk without trying to fix me; I think things would have been very different in my life. I think this is the beauty of restorative justice. The circle is a place of safety, a place of strength for someone who has been victimized. It is a place where the person is allowed to bring their voice to others in a way that the 'harm' is dealt with in a healing fashion. The circle is a place where a person is not labeled 'victim' and therefore is not ascribed with the attributes of victimization such as being weak, vulnerable, and powerless. Rather, the person is seen as a whole person, a person who was victimized, but is not a person to be defined by, and have their entire life defined by that event of victimization."

Voice is a relational experience. When someone is speaking, there is always someone in the circle, who is listening. Voice, in a circle process, is a truth-telling experience. There is no debate about a person's voice in the circle experience. Rather, it is the opportunity for empathy and understanding to find their place in helping repair the harm that has taken place. Voice nurtures the open space for empathy to surface. It does not demand empathy, or demand that empathy be imposed. Voice nurtures and provides us a way to create meaningful, powerful, transformative states.

The fifth element is Sacredness

Over the past 10 years of facilitating training, I regularly hear participants say: 'there was so much respect for everyone in the circle, but I am sure it would not be like this in the real world. This was just a training experience, so everyone was on their best behaviour.' My response to this view is that in a culture that directly or indirectly supports retribution on a daily basis, there is an assumption that people cannot/will not meet in a circle to explore ways to repair harm that has taken place. This assumption is based on a deep belief that either people will be insincere, or that there will be some kind of outburst or exploitation. In other words, many people don't believe that the circle can happen. It is too unrealistic for the "real world."

However, my experience has been, that people are even more deferential in the "real world." Reflecting back on the notion of Koyaanisqatsi, I believe people are very much wanting and seeking another way of living, another way of dealing with the trauma that has come into their lives. The sacredness of the circle is created by everyone in the circle. This is because underneath it all, people, from the very core of their being, began their own story from a place of Goodness. What the circle process does is reinforce the seeking out and experiencing of Goodness. There is a profound caring for others that takes form as the circle process unfolds. I have been witness to people who have come into the circle as "victim" and "offender", hugging each other at the end of the experience. I have been witness to trepidation unfolding into transformation, through the circle process.

I believe that when there is a space that is open enough for the elements of community, capacity, connection, and voice to flourish, all of us evolve into the architects. Together, we can build a sacred space where true transformation can be experienced.

We must be the change in the world, we wish to see.
Gandhi

#65
"Sweat lodge"

The strength within your lodge—your body—speaks of being connected. It is within your body you will find voice. Speak softly, passionately, truthfully, and allow others to hear you.

Conferencing Methodology:

FACILITATOR'S CHECKLIST

1. **Offender:**
   - ☐ acceptance of involvement in the event?
   - ☐ demonstrates remorse?
   - ☐ willingness to make amends in some way to the victim(s)?
   - ☐ would they like someone to be a support for them?
   - ☐ are there police charges?
   - ☐ is this a first offence?
   - ☐ are there bail conditions which would have to be changed before a conference could be held?

2. **Offender's Parents or Guardians:**
   - ☐ are they willing to participate in the process?
   - ☐ are there any other support people that they would like to be a part of the circle?
   - ☐ do they wish the facilitator to speak to their lawyer about the process?

3. **School Administration:**
   - ☐ do they support the use of conferencing in this situation?
   - ☐ other steps have been taken by the school to resolve this issue?
   - ☐ school staff will participate in the circle?
   - ☐ are there other participants they would recommend?
   - ☐ are there any conditions concerning the offender returning to that school that the facilitator should be aware of?

4. **Police:**
   - ☐ do you have a protocol for contacting the investigating officer in the case?
   - ☐ does the officer understand the process and their role in the circle?
   - ☐ are they willing to support the use of a conference?
   - ☐ is there any other information that the facilitator should be aware of (previous charges or warnings or a history with the police)
   - ☐ will the officer take the signed contract back to court at the next appearance?

5. **Victims:**
   ☐   would the victim like an opportunity to tell their side of the story?

   ☐   would they like to face the offender and talk about the impact the harm has caused them?

   ☐   would they like to be part of a solution that will meet everyone's needs?

   ☐   if you work for a school board do you need to have a signed consent to talk to the victim?

   ☐   would it be better if the school principal made the first contact with the victim and their family?

   ☐   do they understand the court process (the time line before a trial and the likely punishment if a guilty verdict is found)?

   ☐   would they like to be part of a pro-active solution in order to feel safe again?

   ☐   do they have an idea of the kind of compensation or solution that would feel right for them?

   ☐   have they names of people they would like to be part of their circle of support?

   ☐   would they need some time to think it over before making a decision?

Conferencing Methodology:

CONFERENCE PREPARATION CHECKLIST

1. **Time**: ☐ have you arranged a time that is suitable for all parties?
[Keep in mind that a conference may take one-two hours to complete.]

☐ are there time lines through the court that you need to be aware?

2. **Location**: ☐ have you booked a room for the conference that will be suitable for a circle format? Is it private?

3. **Format**: ☐ have you briefed everyone involved in the circle as to the format, what the questions will be, and the order of speaking?

4. **Forms and Contracts:**

☐ have you filled out as much information as possible on the forms prior to the conference?

☐ do you have access to a photocopier for the final contract copies to be distributed to the families, police, court, school and your records?

5. **Treats**: ☐ have you purchased cookies and drinks for the close of the circle?
☐ will someone take care of those duties when you leave the room?

6. **Seating plan:**

☐ have you arranged a seating plan for the participants?
☐ are there any interpersonal issues you need to consider in the seating plan?

7. **Conference 'supporter':**

☐ is there someone (i.e. social worker, guidance counsellor) who needs to be part of the follow-up - should be part of the circle even though they are not part of the incident?

Sample Script
The Circle

Step1:

Facilitator: "welcome and thank you for coming to the circle. As you all know my name is (   ). I will be facilitating the circle today. I would first like to underline the reason that we all agreed to be here today and that is: we, all of us, want to participate in a process that can help repair the harm that has taken place. To do this, our circle will be guided by the principles of respect, community and creativity. As we agreed in the meetings prior to this circle, each person will be allowed time to tell how this incident has affected them and what steps can be created to repair what has happened. To this end we have all agreed to hear the voice of each member without interrupting them".

" I would now have each member introduce themselves with the talking stone, beginning with the person to my (   )". Begin this with the person who did the offending behavior.

Step 2:

Once the introductions have been made the facilitator passes the symbol to the person who committed the offending behavior and asks the following:
Name of the individual (   )

- "To begin the process would you tell us how you came to be involved in the event that took place i.e. three weeks ago"

- "What were you thinking, feeling at the time the event took place"?

- " What has been your experience since the event took place leading up to today?"

- "Who have you seen affected by this event?"

At the completion of each of the four questions the facilitator provides a brief pause in order to let the emotion be felt in the circle, without having to fill the silence with words. Now move to the next question. Pauses encourage a sense of calmness in the process. Once the person has answered all four questions, the facilitator thanks the person and has them pass the symbol over to the person who was victimized by the event.

Step 3:

The facilitator now asks the person who was victimized by the event:
Name of the individual (   )

- "Would you tell us how you came to be involved in the event that took place i.e. three weeks ago"?

- "What were you thinking, feeling at the time the event took place?"

- "What has been your experience since the event took place leading up to today?'

- "Who have you seen affected by the event?"

At the completion of the answers, the facilitator thanks the person and asks them to pass the symbol to the supporter sitting beside them.

Step 4:

In sequence beginning with the primary support person of the individual victimized by the event, the person(s) are now asked:

- "Would you tell us how you became involved in the event that took place i.e. three weeks ago?

- "What were you thinking, feeling when you heard about this event?"

- "What has been your experience since this event took place?"

- "Who have you seen affected by this event?"

At the completion of the answers the facilitator asks the supporter of the person victimized by the event to pass the symbol to the next supporter and the same series of questions are asked.

Step 5:

In sequence beginning with members that are supporters of the person who committed the offending behavior they are now asked:

- "Would you tell us how you came to be involved in the event that took place i.e. three weeks ago?

- "What were you thinking, feeling when you heard about this event?"

- "What has been your experience since the event took place?"

- "Who have you seen affected by this event?"

At the completion of the answers the facilitator thanks everyone for their responses.

Step 6:

When all the supporters of the person who committed the offending behavior have responded to the questions, the facilitator receives the symbol and at this juncture states:

"We have had the opportunity to hear from everyone involved in the event and how the event has affected them. Now before looking to the steps that we can create to help repair the harm that has taken place, I would like to ask (the person who did the offending behavior) is there anything you would like to say to anyone in the group". This is often a critical step in the process for the following reasons:

• by this point it can be quite overwhelming for the person who is the offender, for up to this point it is likely the first time that they see just how many people their actions have affected and just how deeply their actions have affected people. Here the feeling of shame can be healthy, or create a defensive posture not only by the individual, but by the supporters of the individual (parents in particular). Asking if there is anything the person would like to say allows for the authentic apology to surface. It is a key element of the process overall.
• it is an opportunity for people to see just who the "offender" is, and that he/she has been affected by the voice, feelings of those who have been victimized by his/her behavior
• this step also sets the context for healthy discussion around what the needs and responsibilities may be in terms of outcomes of the meeting.

Step 7:

Once the person in the offending role offers a comment the facilitator receives the symbol and states:

"Having heard from everyone here today, we will now take the time to hear how everyone can begin to create ways to help repair the harm that has taken place."

Facilitator: Passes the symbol to the person most victimized by the event and asks:

"Having heard from everyone here today what do you need to have happen to help repair the harm?"

Once the person has answered, the facilitator repeats what they have heard as the answer, and may document it in point form in preparation for writing up the agreed-to outcomes. The facilitator thanks the individual and asks them to pass the symbol on to the next person until everyone, with the exception of the person in the role of the offender has offered what their needs are.

Step 8:

The facilitator now passes the symbol to the person in the offender role and asks:

"Having heard from everyone here today, what do you see yourself as being able to do to help repair the harm that has taken place."

The focus of this specific question is on responsibility and capacity. Here the attention is not on the deficiencies of the person but rather on their capacity and responsibility to help make things right.

Once the person has stated what they feel they are capable of doing, the facilitator thanks everyone for their participation and summarizes the agreed-to steps. The facilitator then states:

" The agreed-to outcomes that we have... are they attainable and are they fair? Do they meet peoples' needs and demonstrate responsibilities?" The facilitator takes into account everyone's responses and then states:
" I will take a few minutes to type out the summary, when I return we will go over the agreement and if there are any changes we will make them and sign the agreement. Kindly help yourself to the refreshments while I complete the agreement."

This stage in the process is often where some magic takes place. People simply continue the conversation that has evolved, and at times, new suggestions are created within the spirit of community, respect, and creativity.

It is important that whatever action steps are created, that the people who create those steps are also the ones responsible for carrying them out. It is not necessarily the role of the facilitator to ensure the steps are carried out. The intention here is that the participants are the ones who must ensure maintenance of the needs and responsibilities.

The power of mutually agreed-to outcomes is highlighted in the following way:

1. Of the 100+ circles conducted in the Toronto District School Board, all participants have stated they were satisfied with the outcomes.
2. In contrast, the second most common offence that leads to custody of young offenders are violation of court imposed probation orders.
3. In the circle, it is the participants who create outcomes based on capacity, rather than imposing "orders" aimed at admonishing deficiencies.

Step 9:

Once the agreement is signed, the facilitator takes the symbol and offers the following:
"In bringing the circle to a close I will pass the symbol around to each person and you may make a closing comment if you would like. If you do not wish to make a comment please just say 'pass' and pass the symbol to the person beside you." Begin with the offender, ending with the voice of the person victimized by the event.
The facilitator then takes the symbol and thanks people for their participation.

Post Circle

The facilitator has one other part to their role. Contact, at a pre-arranged date, the persons who have agreed to monitor the outcomes to see if the outcomes have been realized. The facilitator may also advise all participants in the pre-circle stage that there is an evaluation aspect to the circle process. The evaluation piece is simply collecting information on the number of circles that have taken place, the success of the circles (in relation to how people have felt the circle responded to their needs and responsibilities).

#66
"Seven Gather"

"7 men gather around the circle of life, they speak of prophets of yesterday,
today, tomorrow. It is by living in harmony and peace connected to the 4 races
of humanity, it is within that sacred sweat lodge we pray, sing and chant of the
good life we call our path.

Promoting Organizational Change in Response to the YCJA

Kiaras Gharabaghi, Ph.D.
Manager of Residential Resources, Family & Children Services, Waterloo Region

The introduction of the <u>Youth Criminal Justice Act</u> has significantly impacted not only the legal professions in their work with young offenders, but also a wide range of other organizations that have large numbers of young offenders and potential young offenders (also known as *High Risk Youth*) as clients. The Child Welfare system in particular has had to re-evaluate its approach to youth who commit crimes or who are likely to be at risk of committing crimes and who also happen to be in the care of a Children's Aid Society.

Over the course of the past five years, child welfare agencies have had to absorb a number of critical changes, including:

A significant increase in the number of children in care, particularly adolescents

• The introduction of the <u>Safe Schools Act</u>, which has impacted adversely on child welfare clients through increased expulsions/longer term suspensions from schools

• The introduction of the <u>YCJA</u>, which has resulted in youth who have been charged returning to their placements and accumulating additional charges before custody time is imposed

Perhaps even more importantly, however, youth themselves have experienced a major cultural shift in their worldview. Whereas until not long ago, youth viewed the court system, and especially custody, as a place of exclusion, a form of punishment, and 'somewhere you go to be away from society for a while', they now appear to have reversed their view of the criminal justice system generally – custody is very much <u>within</u> their social reality, a place where friends re-unite, where positive relationships with custody staff exist, and an almost mandatory component of any 'cool', 'hip', and culturally relevant youth identity.

Given these concurrent legislative/structural changes on the one hand, and shifts in youth sub-cultures on the other hand, child welfare agencies have been challenged to take stock of a number of long held and deeply embedded assumptions. While some agencies continue to be hesitant in their approach to adjusting to the realities of the <u>YCJA</u>, many other agencies have initiated significant and often difficult dialogue both internally and across agencies within the sector and even across sectors. One such example is *Family & Children Services of Waterloo Region (FACS Waterloo)*, the Children's Aid Society in south-western Ontario responsible for a mostly urban area with an increasingly diverse population of about half a million people. Over the past eighteen months, FACS Waterloo has been pursuing a radically new vision of dealing with the anti-social behaviours of its group home clients in particular.

Many clients in our care have a long history in terms of involvement with the police, the courts, and probation. In most cases, the initial reason for police involvement related to a minor offense, such as theft, mischief, and out of control behaviour. The youth criminal justice system typically responds with probation and related conditions, such as curfews, an order to abide by the rules of the residence, school attendance, and abstinence from drugs and alcohol. For most of the clients who end up with such probation orders, additional charges pile up that are based on the violation of the specific probation orders.

Police involvement is typically viewed as serving a number of purposes:

• Children who break the law should be held responsible for their actions, and legal consequences that would apply to other members of the community should therefore also apply to the children we serve.

• We sometimes struggle with containing the behaviours of some clients, and having the police provide assistance is helpful, even if this often results in an escalation of the child's behaviour followed by charges.

• particular types of behaviours present us with safety concerns that we are ill-equipped to handle; the police are generally able to manage safety concerns more effectively.

• By calling the police, we are able to send clients the message that some types of behaviours will simply not be tolerated. Police officers can speak to the client in ways that we cannot, and therefore, they are more able to provide the client with 'a dose of reality'.

• By involving clients with the court system, we gain valuable resources in terms of ensuring the clients have their needs met; some resources, including various types of assessments, are more easily accessed by the criminal justice system than by us.

Many of these views contain some truth; but none are entirely accurate. The reality is that we work with children and youth who come to us with a wide range of problems, and their actions while living in our group homes are symptomatic of these problems. Our goal is to assist our clients with their problems, and we cannot do this if we do not allow them to openly present their symptoms.

It is extremely important to maintain a clear perspective on the types of problems facing our clients, and what types of behaviours might be reasonable responses from their perspective. Even children who live at home in a nurturing and supportive family environment and who have never experienced any type of hardship engage in difficult and sometimes anti-social behaviours, such as stealing, lying, manipulating, verbal disrespect, violation of curfews, etc. Such children may get into physical fights with peers, throw things at peers and other community members, etc. For the most part, these types of behaviours, while not desirable, are not abnormal either, and in no way are indicative of a criminal mind set. The children we work with in our group homes are subject to all the normal experiences of adolescents, and therefore engage in most of these types of behaviours as well. In addition, they have experienced a great deal of loss, hardship and trauma, which can range from sexual abuse and rape to emotional abuse, neglect, abandonment, loss of family, witness to violence, substance use, etc. Moreover, many are struggling with a wide variety of mental health concerns over which they have no control, including depression, bi-polar disorders, conduct disorders, etc.

Based on this reality, we should fully expect that our clients will not only continue to present the symptoms which may have landed them in care in the first place, but in fact that these symptoms will intensify. Aggression, disrespect, not following the rules, and running away are reasonable responses to the reality these children have to face while living with us.

It is our belief that the children and youth we serve in our group homes are in need of assistance from a supportive and nurturing perspective, rather than punitive interventions. We do recognize that the idea of charging kids for inappropriate and illegal activity, is not without merit. We believe, however, that police involvement is not, at this time, the most effective way of nurturing a change and growth process in our clients.

Having recognized the need to reduce the reliance on police involvement to deal with challenging behaviours on the one hand, and to ensure that youth are nevertheless held accountable for actions that violate the rights of others on the other hand, we now turn our attention to the search for replacements – replacements for the court-based approach we have traditionally used to address these types of issues.

In so doing, we have thus far come to a number of critical conclusions that will undoubtedly change the way we work with 'high risk youth' in our care:

• **Restorative justice** initiatives not only ensure a high level of accountability for the youth, but also provide opportunities for youth in care to contribute positively to the community at large. As such, programs and services that promote public understanding and support for this approach to youth criminal justice are to be commended.

• It will be critical to allow for a re-thinking and perhaps even an awakening of child and youth work as a discipline; for many years now our child and youth workers, who without question have had the greatest impact on the experiences and the decision-making of youth, have worked under the assumption that accountability was synonymous to police involvement and court-based consequences to behaviour. In the process, child and youth work skills were under-utilized and in some cases completely abandoned. Rather than confronting youth about their thinking and decision-making, the discipline has in fact pacified accountability systems through its reliance on external pronouncements of judgment and consequences.

• Managing the anti-social and quasi-criminal behaviours of youth requires much more than a heavy-handed approach by the proxy-parents (child welfare staff). What will undoubtedly be required in the coming years is a multi-disciplinary and multi-sectoral partnership of stakeholders, including formal ones such as crown attorneys, lawyers, police, CAS, probation, schools, etc, and informal ones such as neighbours and neighbourhoods, community centers, recreational resources, and the community at large. Only when we can successfully present to youth a united front in insisting on accountability and responsible citizenship on the one hand, but also a preparedness to actively support, nurture, and coach young people on the other hand, will we be able to meet the philosophical ideals of the new legislation.

The opportunities presented by the introduction of the YCJA are almost too good to be true. For the first time in recent history, there is a non-coercive incentive for all kinds of service sectors to come together in non-traditional partnerships in order to move forward toward a common goal – creating sustainable solutions to the challenges faced by high risk youth and also the challenges faced by the community as a result of the actions taken by high risk youth. The emergence of restorative justice approaches to dealing with youth crime in so many local environments throughout Ontario serves as a strong indication that even the rigidity of the criminal justice system may not in the end suffice to slow the march toward a new, socially meaningful and economically valid way of doing business.

#77
"Sacred Stillness"

It takes a special person to learn to stop. For when one pauses they will find that sacred time, that times in which one communicates, be it in silence of the Way or by the sound of the heart, this is the time of sacred stillness.

The Shame Chair

Rick Owens

It is 10:30 in the morning, and as I step out of my office and into the hall I spot one of the kids from the day treatment program down the hall, sitting slumped down in 'the chair'. He has on his face one of the few expressions I normally see on the faces of the kids who get sent to 'the chair'. For some it is anger, and for others a look of defeat. For him, today, his expression is one of distraction, boredom, distance. He appears to be somewhere else, which makes sense given where he presently sits. There is nothing to do in 'the chair' but see and be seen, and I represent little enough that is of interest to stir him from his reverie.

I have come to refer to this as the shame chair because of its location and the way in which it is used. It is the place to which kids are sent who have somehow shown that they can't manage in class in the way that is expected. It is the place kids go to wait, to serve time, and eventually to "process" their transgressions with a staff member. It is out in the hall, one of the busiest areas of the building – visible to all who are on their way to one of the many offices, the kitchen, meeting rooms and washrooms. In the shame chair, the kids are on display for workers like me or visitors, for both the foreign and the familiar. We are all witnesses to their punishment.

As I near the washroom, he looks up and we make eye contact. He is almost 17 years old and is one of my favourite kids in the building. He acknowledges me and I, contrary to the wishes of some staff in his program, greet him. I resist the urge to walk over the remaining 25 feet to say a proper hello and ask him what it was that led to him being sent to the chair. My compromise, though, is that I don't do more than say hello as I continue on to my destination. His time in the chair is intended to be solitary, despite the busyness of the location. We must all – but he more than any – resist the natural urge to talk. The other urge I feel is to release him from the chair, to send him back to class or even outside to take a walk or go for a smoke – anything but sitting on display like a thief in the stocks in the town square or the comic strip kid sitting in the corner with the DUNCE cap on.

This is what we sometimes do to children who have not learned to govern their behaviour in a manner consistent with our standards. These are the kids whose conduct has crossed some invisible and often shifting line of social expectations. These are also the children whose bodies betray them in those moments and places where the most is expected. What is ironic is that, next to them, we are the ones who ought to know best what it must be like to try to contain and control the inattention and impulsivity that come with ADD and ADHD, the tics that come with Tourette's Syndrome, the social and intellectual struggles that come with an intellectual disabilities and developmental disorders. Despite our experience and "expertise", we are sometimes among those whose 'teachable moments' are transformed into episodes of shaming and embarrassment. What makes this all the more appalling is that the chair – our chair – is an event piled on top of these children's often extensive histories of being teased, shamed, chastised and tormented by peers, classmates, brothers and sisters, and other people in positions of authority.

That we have come to rest so comfortably in a professional place that includes 'the chair' suggests that we have forgotten what it is like to be singled out from amongst one's classmates and sent to sit apart from the group. We have not stopped to imagine (or, for some, remember) what it must be like to sit on display out in the hall in front of so many others. We have stopped imagining and employing other ways of dealing with the inevitable misbehaviours and social stumbling of the children with whom we work.

Melissa Orlie[1] uses the term "trespass" to refer to those inevitable instances when our engagement with another causes harm or ill effects, often disguised as 'helping'. These transgressions are contained in even the most (seemingly) benign gestures as offering a bowl of soup to a homeless man who is hungry. Using Orlie's notion of trespass, Amy Rossiter[2] describes how in the gesture of giving soup is produced both the kindly giver and the needy recipient. The homeless man is produced as one whose need is satisfied by the generosity of the well-intentioned volunteer, not as one who is receiving what is rightfully his (were this a part of the world and time in history in which it was every person's right to be properly fed).

In the hallway, the boy sits in his chair because a well-meaning worker has sent him there. Like the volunteer with soup, she is not a bad person; on the contrary, she cares quite deeply about the young people entrusted to her care. But in her good intentions is a "trespass" that has effects for the boy who sits in the chair. Where she fails – where so many of us fail – is in recognizing in our acts the trespasses against the people we are committed to helping.

June Price Tangney, a Professor of Psychology who has researched and written extensively about shame and guilt, argues that interventions or actions that cause a person to feel shame usually produce the opposite responses to those that were sought. With the shame chair as an example, we can reasonably assume that the worker who sent the boy to sit in the hall was, in addition to trying to keep him from disturbing and frustrating others (often including the staff members, too), hoping to get him to reflect on and possibly even change his behaviour. What is more likely evoked, however, is not the development of a sense of guilt – which Tangney and Dearing[3] argue is a useful and productive emotion because of the degree to which it is about a sense of the impact of one's *behaviour* on *others* – but a sense of shame, which they suggest has more to do with feeling bad about one's *self*. In the end, sending the boy to the shame chair is much more likely to make him feel bad about who he is rather than what he did, which goes against all that we are trying to achieve in our work with children who struggle in school.

The term "iatrogenesis" is used most often in the field of medicine to refer to instances where a symptom or illness is actually caused by the treatment. I believe that it has some application to those situations where our ways of working in so-called 'helping' relationships with people end up causing some of the emotional wounds and reactions that we are quick to attribute to the range of struggles that many children with complex needs experience in their communities and families. In his 1996 book, *Beyond Discipline: From Compliance to Community*, Alfie Kohn challenges those of us who work with children in learning environments – arguably every social space, when you think about it – to look at the ways in which we, the so-called 'grown-ups', elicit and make the behaviours for which we punish children. Again, thinking of the shame chair, we have to ask ourselves what the existence and use of that chair tells us about that classroom, that school, and the school systems in which so many of our children are enrolled. We might also want to ask ourselves what it is that we really think the chair accomplishes. We can be sure of what it doesn't accomplish – the development of a classroom community in which children get to 'do' community the way they get to 'do' math and spelling.

Several months after writing down some of my thoughts about the shame chair, we began gradually training most of the staff in our organization about the values and practices associated with restorative justice. In one of the early trainings, Art and Lynn made reference to the shame chair that I had told them about, and I began to worry about how some of my colleagues might react to my characterization of the chair and its effects for kids. Although we didn't discuss it at length in the training, I bumped into the supervisor of the program a day or two later and we stopped to talk about the chair (which was, ironically, occupied as we spoke). When I had first broached the topic of the chair a few months before, the response to my invitation to eliminate the chair was answered with a simple question that I couldn't immediately answer: "OK, but what would you have us do instead?" As we spoke again, months later and so soon after the supervisor had attended the restorative practices training, our conversation shifted from one of "IF" to one about "WHEN".

In the many months that have followed, there have been changes, both subtle and obvious. The chair disappeared at the end of the school year and did not reappear at the start of the next. Several months into the school year, near the end of the first term, the chair reappeared, but this time it was positioned behind a desk, and both were placed around the corner and out of site of people traveling the halls. My surprise and concern were apparent when I next saw the supervisor and asked about the reappearance of the chair. I learned that the desk and chair were used by students, not as a form of punishment, but as a place of escape. Whenever a student feels the need to get away from the group and have some time to himself, he can simply excuse himself and go around the corner to what is, in effect, a more private work space. Perhaps we will come to call it the "tranquility chair."

(Footnotes)
[1] See Orlie, M. (1997). *Living Living Ethically, Acting Politically*. Ithaca, N.Y.: Cornell University Press.
[2] This example is taken from a powerful article by Amy Rossiter which can be found in the Spring 2001 edition of *Critical Social Work* (http://www.criticalsocialwork.com)
[3] Tangney, J. Price & Dearing, R.L. (2002) *Shame and Guilt*. New York: The Guilford Press.

Adaptations & Accommodations Working Toward Inclusion

Rick Owens

It is too often assumed that those who have complex needs such as mental health problems, intellectual disabilities, developmental disorders, learning and communication disorders are not capable of participating in processes through which they are invited to take responsibility for the effects of their actions. 'He doesn't know any better' or 'She didn't really know what she was doing' reflect assumptions about the capacity of some people to understand, reflect on and take responsibility for their actions. It also underestimates the ability of communities to communicate in straight-forward ways how they have been affected by what someone has done, and to articulate their needs. More than anything, though, these assumptions can sometimes rob those with complex needs of opportunities to take responsibility for their actions and repair the harm they may have caused.

In my experience, it is the exception when someone cannot appreciate their impact on others and, in some way, participate in the process of making things right. Time after time I have been reminded not just that people with complex needs *can* participate in RJ conferences, but that they also *want* to. This is also true for those people with complex needs who are among those affected by the actions of another. What has been required has usually been little more than simple adaptations of the process to ensure that all participants are able to attend, participate in and understand what is being said and done.

In the following pages, I'll look at some of the different barriers to participation that some people may face, and suggest some ways in which restorative justice conferences and circles[1] can be adapted to work for most people. I say "most" because restorative justice conferences are not going to work for everyone and will not be appropriate to all situations. There will be people for whom the process is too distressing, premature or too complicated, and there will be situations in which one or more parties have no interest in meeting face-to-face with the person who harmed them. Finally, as we have learned from those working in forensic psychology and psychiatry, there are some people for whom the experience of listening to others recounting their experiences of victimization may be pleasurable rather than healing.

> *The incident was a simple one, and familiar to any who have grown up where there is winter. Two boys outside school between classes are throwing snowballs. One of the two tires of the game and says that he wants to stop; the other isn't quite ready to stop and keeps throwing snow balls. Then, the first boy becomes frustrated and threatens to get the other boy in trouble, which is answered by one last snowball which, as it happens, had a piece of ice in it. The snowball hits its target in the stomach and he falls to the ground crying. When members of the school staff intervene, the 'victim' demands that the police be called, and they are.*

The 'offender' is charged with assault and the matter moves into the youth justice system.

This would, on the surface of it, appear to be a situation in which a restorative justice conference might make a great deal of sense, except for the fact that the two boys attend a treatment program for youth with complex mental health problems. Each has at least 4 diagnoses, including Anxiety Disorder, Attention Deficit/Hyperactive Disorder, Conduct Disorder, Obsessive Compulsive Disorder, etc. In talking with the boys' parents and workers I learn that neither is able to sit in meetings for more than 15 or 20 minutes without getting either very restless or very angry. Neither likes novelty or strangers very much, and one of them – the 'offender' – is prone to explosive behaviour and being verbally abusive when he gets agitated (which reportedly comes easily and often).

Although it has taken 6 months to get to the point where the youth court is prepared to resolve this matter, the timing couldn't have been better. Several months before, we[2] had initiated the development of a restorative justice network that was designed to specialize in using restorative practices and conferencing in situations involving youth with complex needs[3]. The model entails training staff who specialize in working with youth who have complex needs to be restorative justice conference facilitators. This combination of skills and experiences ensures that any preparations and accommodations that the youth might need can be made, both in anticipation of and during the conference. This was our first referral and would be my first conference.

I was a bit unnerved by the descriptions of the boys that I was getting from staff members and family, but I was most struck by the focus on incapacity.

- *'He can't sit still that long.'*
- *'He gets too anxious.'*
- *'He gets too angry.'*
- *'He's not good with strangers.'*
- *'You know he's OCD/ODD/ADHD/PDD'*

Everything I was told suggested that both boys would have great trouble participating in a restorative justice conference, but both boys insisted that they could and would do it.

I described for the boys what a conference might look like and asked them each what they might need or could do to make a long meeting (by which I meant 90 minutes or more) possible. One boy suggested that he would have an easier time focusing on the meeting if he was allowed to bring his Yu-Gi-Oh! cards[4] and play with them. He also explained that he is able to tell when he is starting to get frustrated, and that he would give me the agreed upon signal if he needed to take a break. The other boy suggested that doodling makes him feel better and might help him to focus. Both indicated that they would rather sit at a table than in an open circle, and that they would each like to bring a parent.

In spite of the predictions of some people that the conference would fail, both boys managed to stay focused and to contribute for nearly two hours. We had to take only one break due to frustration, and both boys demonstrated a remarkable degree of maturity and compassion. The boy who had been hit by the snowball was able to acknowledge that the roles have sometimes been reversed and that he has sometimes been the aggressor. The boy who threw the snowball was able to acknowledge the impact of what he had done, but to also highlight how he has suffered too as a result of his actions. What was especially impressive was that he managed to talk about the effects for him in a manner that took nothing away from his classmate's experience. And the parents did a beautiful job of talking about their shared experiences of raising a child with "special needs."

In the end, the group generated one of the most creative and appropriate agreements I have seen, before or since. The 'victim' and his parents insisted that there be no consequences for the other boy, because his involvement in the youth justice system had proved to be a significant consequence on its own. The boys agreed to apologize, each for their transgressions over the years, and to make a greater effort to get along in the future. They also agreed to report back to the staff in their program about the conference and its outcome. But what was most remarkable was the parents' in building the capacity of the school program to deal with future conflicts. It was their wish that staff in the program would be able to offer all of their students a way of resolving conflicts without necessarily involving the youth justice system. They asked that the agreement stipulate that I was to offer restorative justice conference facilitation training to at least one staff member in the program, and to invite that program to join our restorative justice Network. I was struck by the simplicity and sophistication of their agreement, but even more so by their ability to identify the true problem – the school program needed to have a suitable response available to the students for those inevitable instances when they came into conflict.

The following are some of the perceived barriers to participation with which some conference and circle participants may struggle. Although it may be a statement of the obvious, you should note that few of the categories and struggles noted in this discussion are discrete and distinct. Different people experience different manifestations and constellations of effects and so each person must be seen and treated as unique.

Intellectual Disabilities[5]

Still sometimes formally referred to as "mental retardation", this refers to a broad and permanent cognitive impairment that affects a person's learning, thinking and adaptive skills. Affecting approximately 3% of the population, nearly 9 out of ten of all people with an intellectual disability fall within what is referred to as the "mild range". This means that although they very likely struggle with complicated learning and work tasks, they can still be active and often independent participants in the community. They work, go to school and can have a rich social life. Their intellectual abilities may limit their options in terms of schooling and vocations, but, despite some of the myths and assumptions to the contrary, people with intellectual disabilities still have the ability to tell right from wrong, to recognize when they have been harmed by another or when their actions have been the cause of harm.

Although each person is unique in their capacities and struggles, there are some fairly common struggles for people with an intellectual disability.

Time

One of the most complicated yet taken-for-granted concepts in the dominant culture is time. Time is essentially an abstraction that we ground in everyday experience through a variety of means. Most of us learned in childhood to use watches and clocks to measure the passage of time. Young children who have yet to learn how to use clocks can still quantify the passage time through reference to events that take up predictable amounts of time, such as recess at school (fifteen minutes), or events that happen at predictable times (when their favourite show starts.) For some people, though, questions about "when, "how long" or "how much time" may not be well grounded in units such as minutes and hours. So, a question about how long something took may elicit a response that doesn't seem to make sense to those of us who have developed what feels like a 'natural' sense of time. In actuality, our 'natural' sense of time likely has more to do with having had abstractions like a 'minute' or an 'hour' grounded in experiences that we have repeated hundreds or thousands of times.

What is helpful for those who may not yet have developed a concrete sense of units of time is to provide that grounding or reference in everyday experience. So, for example, when asking questions of 'how long', you might want to use cultural references for which there are generally predictable durations with beginnings and ends, such as: a TV commercial (approximately 30 seconds), how long it takes to brush your teeth (a couple of minutes), a TV show (an episode of The Simpson's is 30 minutes long), or a movie (usually 90 to 120 minutes), and so on. If you are familiar with the person's routines, you may be able to use examples such as how long it takes them to walk to the bus stop or the local store. Using concrete examples such as this enables you to check with someone about their sense of time with a question like, "When you say it took 'a while', do you mean as long as _____? To explore questions about "when" something took place, you may want to give examples of significant times of day or routine events (e.g. lunch time), days of the week, seasons, or special occasions ("Was it before summer started or after?")

Memory

Obviously related to time are our memories of events. The recollection of things past is not, as we often assume, a simple, single-step exercise. My memory today of something that happened even yesterday is dependent upon ability to take in and make sense of the event at the time, my ability to retrieve that memory from among the millions of potential memories I have 'stored' in my head, and to communicate that memory to another person by providing a coherent narrative that is situated in time. That complexity helps to explain, if only in part, why it is difficult for many of us, but especially for some people with an intellectual disability, to answer the seemingly simple question, "What happened?"

While it is ideal that a conference be held as soon after the transgression as possible

– to ensure that the events are still relatively 'fresh' in the minds of those involved – it is not uncommon for months to have passed and memories to have faded. In talking to someone who has harmed another we can sometimes almost reflexively greet statements like, "I don't know" with disbelief, but it is important to keep in mind that this may be quite sincere and reflect very real struggles to recall events. You should watch for signs that the person from whom you are trying to elicit the story or answer may be feeling embarrassment or frustration. As a facilitator, it will be important for you to be patient and offer encouragement, without being patronizing. You can assist sometimes by reminding the speaker of the time of year, the location, or of other significant events that may have occurred at around the same time ("Remember that it happened just after school started." or "That was the day that the police came to see you at your house."). You might want to encourage them to turn to their support person if s/he is someone who is experienced with helping them to recollect their experiences (e.g. "I remember that there had been a big snow storm that day."). Finally, you may want to offer to come back to them later in the process so that they can be helped by the recollections of other participants. Some participants may simply find it easier to reconstruct their story in response to that told by another participant.

Feelings

We make many assumptions about feelings, both in how they are experienced and about how they are interpreted. We forget sometimes that we don't all experience the same feelings under the same circumstances, and even that our feelings aren't always obvious to others. When we take into account the powerful cultural norms, the biochemistry, neurological development (think even of the changes taking place in the brain during childhood and adolescence) the cognitive processes, and the intricacies of coming to shared understandings about feelings, we can better recognize why it is that our feelings are so often a part of conflict and miscommunication. We each struggle with the complexities of emotions – in expressing ours in appropriate and effective ways, and understanding and responding to those of others – but for people with an intellectual disability there are even greater challenges.

Some people with intellectual disabilities may have difficulty recognizing and communicating about their own feelings. It may be difficult for them to understand some of the ways in which we intellectualize and articulate feelings, especially with respect to more subtle feelings that fall outside of the central trinity of happy, mad, and sad. This means that we have to be careful not to assume that everyone understands what we mean when we talk feelings such as 'embarrassment' or 'irritation'. In some instances, a person may have particular difficulty interpreting non-verbal communication such as the expression on our face or the tone of someone's voice. This means that a person could be saying "I'm not bothered" with a facial expression and tone that communicate anything but contentment, but it would be the verbal elements that register.

Where this might prove to be problematic in a restorative justice exercise is when one person does not appear to recognize and appreciate the feelings that another participant is showing or discussing. It may also be somewhat perturbing for some participants when another says, "I don't know" when asked about how they were or are feeling. It is important for the facilitator to sometimes assist participants with the non-verbal as well as the verbal communication. You may need to spend a bit more time helping some participants to put their feelings into words or to understand those being expressed or described by others. It may also be necessary for the facilitator to 'language' or put the non-verbal expression of feelings – facial expressions, tone of voice, etc. – into words so that all participants understand what is being communicated.

One last point about feelings: We often throw around the term 'empathy' as though pretty much everyone – except perhaps psychopaths – can and should have it. In truth, it requires a set of complex meta-cognitive (essentially, thinking about thinking) and social skills that we each may possess in varying degrees. It is unfair, however, to assume that everyone can and should be able to understand the feelings in themselves that are being evoked as you take in the experience of another, and then communicate that understanding back to them. The truth is that relatively few of us are actually very good at empathy, so seeking some degree of empathy as an outcome of a restorative justice conference or circle may not be fruitful. Instead, what we should be more often looking to develop is a level of understanding or recognition, especially of the harm that has been caused.

Communication

In the section above, I talked about understanding and communicating feelings. In this section the focus is on communication through verbal language. Put simply, it is essential that the facilitator makes sure that all participants understand what is being said, that everyone has enough time to think about and formulate their responses, and that everyone is using language that the others can understand. This is where the ability to pause and slow down the process may be especially helpful. To be clear, though, this is not about talking down to someone; rather, it is ensuring that you have a shared understanding of what is being communicated.

Few of us like to reveal our limitations, so we should anticipate that a person with an intellectual disability is not usually going to be keen to admit to his limitations or spontaneously point out that he doesn't understand something another person has said. Instead, it will sometimes fall to the facilitator to check in with all participants to make sure that they are understanding what is being said, and to assume the need for explanation or elaboration when someone is using complex language or speaking in abstractions. When someone uses a complicated word or concept that you suspect may not be understood by one or more of the participants, you may want to politely interrupt, suggest that we each sometimes use words in different ways, and then ask them to explain what they mean when they use that word or term. You could also say something like, "When I use that word I usually mean____. Is that what you mean when you say it?"

Some forms of communication can be especially complicated, such as sarcasm and irony. These sophisticated forms of humour can be difficult for some people to follow and can lead to misunderstandings rather than clarity. Watch, too, for the use of abstractions in the form of metaphors, analogies and idioms. Expressions such as, "It was as easy as pie" or "I was down in the dumps" rarely cross cultures and, if taken literally, could be very confusing for some participants. Given the goal of achieving a shared understanding, it may be worthwhile asking the speaker to explain what they mean.

Although many people with an intellectual disability will struggle with some of the limitations outlined above (and others not discussed herein) it is essential that we remember that each person has strengths as well as limitations. It is likely that any person with an intellectual disability that you are working with is able to do some things well, and you may even find that they don't seem to have a disability. Sometimes referred to as "cloaking", people with intellectual disabilities learn how to conceal their limitations and thereby avoid the mistreatment to which they are too often exposed throughout their lives. It is also important to remember that there is a much greater likelihood that someone with an intellectual disability has been victimized than offended, and that those who has been identified as the "offender" will quite likely have their own experiences as a victim. This is not mentioned to excuse or even explain anyone's behaviour, but to highlight the complexity of the lives of those you might encounter in your work as a facilitator.

Emotional and Behavioural Struggles

Psychiatric diagnoses and labels are complex, highly contested and sometimes very helpful descriptions of sets of behaviours that people exhibit. Although many of the people with complex needs that I have worked with have had diagnoses, many have not. And, given that many behaviours fit multiple diagnostic categories or are simply not unique to people who have identified mental health problems – many of us manifest some of these behaviours at least some of the time – I will, in the pages that follow, look not at the diagnoses themselves but at some of the feelings and behaviours that can complicate a person's experiences, including their involvement in restorative justice conferences.

Restlessness/Inattention

In recent decades, much has been made of Attention Deficit Disorder (ADD) and Attention Deficit Hyperactivity Disorder (ADHD). While these describe very real struggles and related behaviours, these labels like many others are not always helpful. In addition to reducing sometimes very complex experiences down to a diagnostic label, these terms imply a sort of dichotomy – one either does or doesn't 'have' the disorder. In truth, however, we all fit somewhere on a complex continuum between two poles. At the one end are those who cannot concentrate or sit still for any length of time and for whom stimulant medications are often quite helpful. These are the people who in schools may be unable to stay focused on their work, distract others and seem to be in constant motion. These are also the people who may be able to do two things at once, such as doing their homework while watching television or listening to music. At the other end of the continuum are those who may be able focus for hours at a time on activity despite the presence of distractions. Someone with this ability may be able to read a book while surrounded by others who are talking, seeming to be able to shut out all that is going on around them.

It is worth noting that despite its prevalence amongst children, not all restlessness and inattention is attributable to ADD/ADHD. These behaviours may be caused by a range of physiological and psychological phenomena, including emotional trauma, anxiety and even depression. Regardless of the origins of the behaviours it is important to keep in mind that they are rarely intentional, and that simple steps can be taken to adapt restorative justice conferences to accommodate people who struggle with staying focused and settled for as long as a conference or circle might take.

If you think back to the story at the start of this chapter, in which the two boys both struggled with staying focused in long meetings, you may recall that both boys were asked what they can do to help themselves stay focused. Although relatively young, both boys could easily describe activities that they knew were effective for them. The one boy chose to doodle while the other sorted his trading cards. What was integral to the success of this conference was that both boys were asked by the facilitator what they could and should do, they were encouraged to bring the items they needed, and they were encouraged to use the items during the meeting. What was especially important, however, was that their strategies were shared and explained with the rest of the participants at the start of the conference. Everyone knew from the outset that the doodling and the cards were what enabled the boys to listen better, to participate more, and to remain in the circle for what were actually remarkable lengths of time. Used without explanation, the boys' activities might have been perceived as quite disrespectful, but having the boys explain what they were doing allowed us all to recognize and honour the effort they put in to staying in the circle.

When preparing participants for a conference, I make sure to ask them what they are like in meetings and what meetings are like for them. Do they get restless or can they manage to sit in a meeting for as long as a couple of hours? What happens when they start to get bored? How can others tell when they are feeling restless or bored? If there are parents, care providers or staff members involved in the preparation meeting, it may be helpful to ask them what they think the participant might need to have or do in order to stay focused in the conference. You may want to encourage participants to select and bring items or activities that won't be too consuming or especially distracting to others in the conference. The trading cards and doodling worked because they were sufficiently engaging to help the participants, but not so much so that they became engrossed in them, or so disturbing that others weren't able to focus. It may also be useful to acknowledge at the start of the conference that most of us get restless at some point in long meetings, and that we each handle it in different ways. To normalize this reaction, I sometimes point out that one of the ways in which I deal with restlessness is to play with my pen or a small stone that I carry in my pocket. And finally, in recognition of the fact that most activities or distractions – like the cards or doodling or my rock – have limited utility, it is important to also build in a break and to invite people to ask for one if they are feeling the need to get up and move around.[6]

Anxiety

The prospect of sitting for hours in a room filled with people you may not know and that you have somehow wronged – or have been wronged by – is surely enough to intimidate the most confident among us. If you then imagine that everyone is coming together to talk about the most shameful thing you have ever done, that you are only 15 years old, and that whatever comes of this meeting might be shared with a Youth Court, you can begin to see how some participants might be nearly overwhelmed with worry.

Given that most people participating in a restorative justice conference will likely be doing so for the first time, it is probably reasonable to assume that virtually everyone will be at least a little bit nervous in the beginning. One of the important aspects of the conference model described in chapter __ of this manual is the inclusion of support people. Anyone attending a conference is invited to bring a support person, which will likely be of considerable comfort for most people. Similar to the points made above, you may also want to invite anxious participants to bring along an object that is soothing or comforting for them.

There is, in fact, much that can be done prior to the conference to reduce participants' anxiety, chief among these is to be very clear with every participant that they have a choice about attending. No one should feel forced to participate in a restorative justice conference, not even the person who has been identified as the 'offender'. We don't assume that everyone will want to participate and, especially in situations where a participant has complex needs, we don't ask them if they will until they have had a chance to hear about what a conference looks and feels like, how it is structured, and what sorts of outcomes are possible. Their decisions must be informed decisions.

As a part of helping participants to prepare for conferences, I will often provide them with a script or list of the questions that they will be asked, along with an outline of the process. This enables them to anticipate what they will be asked and even plan what they will say, which eliminates most of the surprises that might arise. It also enables participants more time to reflect and, if necessary, to jog their memory, which is especially helpful in situations where considerable time has passed. Participants who may struggle with reading in English are encouraged to go over the outline with a support person who can help them to understand the written material and reflect on and even write down their experiences and possible answers.

One very anxious and soft-spoken young man who had been beaten up by another youth at school was invited to participate in a restorative justice conference six months later. At the end of our initial conversation he indicated that he was not quite sure if he felt confident and comfortable enough to attend. I suggested to him that he take a few days to think about it and to talk it over with his mother before answering. When I spoke to him a few days later, he said that he would likely not come but would instead send his mother to speak on his behalf. We spoke on the phone every few days as we tried to work out the details for the conference and how they would get there from the town to which they had moved at the end of the school year. Each time I spoke to him he took a 'step' closer to the conference. "I'll come to the city, but I won't come to the conference." "I'll come to the building, but I won't come in the room." Finally, just a couple of days before we were to meet, he said, "I'll come into the room, but my mom will do the talking."

On the morning of the conference, the young man showed me that he had typed out his story for his mother to read on his behalf. When we began I directed the first question to him, feeling that it was respectful to begin that way, but fully expecting that his mother would provide the answer. Before she could respond, the young immediately answered the first question, and then the next and the next without once turning to his mother or even referring to his notes. At the end of the conference, as I made my closing remarks, I wondered aloud at how he had managed to, not only to be at the conference but to participate without the help of his mother or his notes. The young man was beaming with pride and stood to offer his hand to the boy who had assaulted him.

The story that opened this chapter is also instructive, in that the two boys both asked that we use a table instead of sitting in an open circle. One of the advantages of an open circle is the openness that it represents and requires, but for these two boys, the vulnerability and openness was too provocative. Their anxiety was such that they were better able to participate across the safety of a table. What is common to both of these examples is that the participants not only knew in advance what the conference would look like, they were also given the opportunity to shape the process. In both instances, their adaptations enabled them to participate and took nothing away from the process or outcome.

Anger and Frustration

When the referral came in from the Court I was surprised. The boy that was being referred for a restorative justice conference was someone I had met before and, while I hardly knew him, I was aware of his tendency to fly into a rage with the slightest provocation (he had, in fact, slammed a door in my face, though I think the incident was far more memorable – and exceptional – for me than it had been for him). He had been diagnosed with several disorders, the most obvious of which were Intermittent Explosive and Antisocial Personality Disorders, neither of which made him easy to be around. Although I was reticent about conducting a conference with him (he had assaulted a worker in his group home and had not been at all remorseful, as far as anyone knew) the Assistant Crown Attorney was convinced that this was the best thing to do, under the circumstances.

I invited the young man, his therapist and his residence worker (not the one he had assaulted) to meet with me to talk about the referral and what a conference might be like. Within only a few minutes, the young man had slipped into profanity and name-calling, directed at all of us who were present and at the worker who was the 'victim' in the matter we were discussing. I ended the meeting, suggesting that we each needed to give some thought to whether it was a good idea to proceed.

I contacted the staff at the court and learned that the Assistant Crown Attorney was strongly urging us to find a way to include this youth in a restorative justice conference. The staff at the group home and his counsellor both said that they knew that he would probably get some benefit from the experience, but that they also acknowledged that he would likely become verbally abusive with the 'victim', which was something none of us could reasonably permit. The youth's therapist then went on to talk about what it is that triggers this young man's rages. I already knew that the young man had a dual diagnosis[7], but the therapist suggested that the youth had a pronounced problem with taking in and processing language. This meant that most conversations exceeded his ability to keep up after the first few sentences, which, the therapist surmised, was a source of considerable frustration and embarrassment. The easiest way for the young man to conceal his difficulty with comprehension was to distract everyone in a way that ended the conversation. The one thing he had learned to use to great effect was his temper.

What this suggested to me was that the young man needed a chance to take in what was being said at his own pace. He needed time to process it, to develop a response and then finally to articulate it. And he needed to do it without an audience, which pretty much eliminated a conventional restorative justice conference process. Although it seemed to go against so much of what a restorative justice conference stands for – bringing a person together with those who have been affected by his actions, to hear from and address each other, and to come to some agreement about how to repair the harm – I proposed that we conduct the conference by e-mail. This would enable the young man the time and space he needed to process what he was 'hearing' from others, and to articulate his own thoughts without becoming enraged. We all agreed to give it a try.

When the first e-mail came back from the young man, I was concerned that his residential counsellor had not followed my instructions. The young man's responses were thoughtful, articulate, and betrayed a surprising insight into both his behaviour and its impact on others, especially the 'victim' in this matter. I called the worker to ask him if he had followed my instructions to record only what the young man said, and to not influence his responses in any way. The worker reassured me that the words in the e-mail were the young man's; there had been no prompting or coaching. I was amazed.

I have little doubt that this young man will have further conflict with the law, and will offend – and perhaps offend against – many more people in his time. But what the conference provided was a chance for all of us, especially the young man, to have a different experience of him. With some fairly simple and admittedly unorthodox adaptations to the restorative justice conference process, the young man was able to come out from behind his defenses and give us each a very rich glimpse of his capacity for insight, reflection, and sensitivity.

What is sought in a restorative justice process is a chance for participants to say what their thoughts, feelings and experiences were, to feel that they were heard, and to participate in repairing at least some of the harm that has been done. It is generally understood that this, like democracy, can be a bit messy but that it is very often worthwhile. In the example described above, my concern was that the process not lead to any greater harm, and at the point where it seemed to me that we could proceed without the risk of doing greater harm than good, we went ahead. There was, in a sense, a cost-benefit analysis in which we had to weigh the potential benefits for participants against the possibility of further harm. In this instance we were able to control for the harm; his responses came to me first and would only be sent to the 'victim' after I was sure that the youth's correspondence didn't have the same flavour as what he generally ended up saying in person. In actuality, though, it is not always possible to anticipate or control for the anger that may arise.

It is almost inevitable that anger will emerge in some form and to some degree during a restorative justice conference. These are, after all, situations in which people are invited to talk about something harmful that happened, and to reflect on what feelings were evoked during and following the incident. It is useful, therefore, to have a good sense of what your feelings are about anger and its expression. It is helpful, too, to know where your comfort ends and concern begins when others are obviously angry.

A part of what makes the restorative justice conferencing model described in this book so effective is the degree to which the meetings are structured. This structure creates a degree of containment which, along with some confidence in the facilitator's abilities, enables participants to feel safer. But a part of good preparation for conferences, especially when one or more participants may have complex needs, is to screen for vulnerability to the anger of others, and tendencies that any participants might have to lose control of their temper. Although anger is a very healthy and normal emotion, especially in situations where one person has harmed another, we must be cognizant of that threshold between benefits and harm.

I have often asked prospective participants if they have any worries about anger, theirs or others'. When participants suggest that they sometimes have problems with their own anger, I ask them if the can tell when they are getting angry, and if there are ways that others might be able to tell. In some situations, such as in the story that opened this chapter, I have found it useful to build in signals for participants to indicate that they might need a break. I have also stopped conferences to insert a break where I have perceived the need. I have even ended a conference altogether, when it became apparent that we had reached the benefit/harm threshold. This was, however, the exception, and the vast majority of conferences go quite well when there has been adequate planning and preparation.

The Toronto Restorative Justice Network: A Model for Inclusion[8]

The preceding examples and suggestions are by no means an exhaustive list of the barriers to and accommodations for participation in restorative justice conferences. My intent has been to offer some sense of the sorts of issues and behaviours that may arise in working with participants with complex needs, and to encourage you to think broadly and creatively about how to make it possible for them to participate. Some of what I have described will seem intimidating, especially for the reader who is new to restorative practices and, perhaps, to working with people who have complex needs. The truth is that it can be very challenging. Although there is great comfort in working with an established structure and even with a script, no two conferences are alike, and the introduction of complex needs into the mix does, I believe, necessitate that the facilitator have some additional specialized skills.

In recognition of the need for both restorative justice conference facilitation skills and the ability to recognize and attend to the unique struggles of participant's with complex needs, we have developed what we are calling a 'network model'. To ensure that there are restorative justice conference facilitators in our area who are able to include young persons[9] with complex needs, we have enlisted experienced staff from a number of agencies in the city to participate in three days of intensive training. The goal of the training is to supplement their existing skills and experiences in working with people who have complex needs with facilitations skills, so that when a situation arises, someone from one of the

Network partner agencies can be called on to serve as a facilitator.

The network model is especially effective in circumstances where attention must be paid to perceptions and experiences of impartiality. If, for example, there is a situation in one agency – such as the snowball incident described at the start of the chapter – the staff in that agency may not be the best people to respond, because they may be asked to attend the conference as either supporters or as participants who have been affected. What that agency can, then, do is contact the Network and ask that a trained facilitator – who is also experienced in working with a similar client population – be invited in to convene a conference.

Among the other advantages of the network model is that there is a larger pool of trained facilitators[10] who can consult with each other or, when necessary, to pair up and co-facilitate conferences. This is especially helpful in the early stages of a facilitator's development, when it may be comforting for the novice to invite someone with more experience to serve as their co-facilitator, consultant or support person. Establishing a network also enables the development of a range of specializations within the pool. Within the TRJN there are agencies and facilitators who, for example, are specialized primarily in working with youth who have an intellectual disability or a developmental disorder, while others have more experience in working with street involved youth. Some facilitators are more familiar with day programs, while others are more experienced with sexual abuse treatment programs. The larger the network the greater the potential is for a diversity and wealth of experiences in other areas too, such as with different languages and ethno-cultural communities. We have also trained staff who have a wealth of experience in working with LGBTT[11] youth and in the areas of sexuality and sexual identity.

Summary

The central goals and values of restorative practices are about the building and maintenance of communities, and the inclusion of all those who are willing to be members of those communities. What I hope I have demonstrated in this chapter is that many of those who are marginalized in our communities, and in the justice systems, can and should be included. One of the many ways in which we can accomplish this inclusion is through restorative justice conferences and circles that are adapted to accommodate the needs and strengths of people with complex needs, such as mental health problems, intellectual disabilities, developmental disorders, learning and communication disorders. The adaptations described in this chapter are by no means an exhaustive list of what can be done when we are creative and work with participants to make conferences and restorative practices work for them. I have mentioned only a handful of the sorts of struggles faced by people with complex needs. Given the variety of 'disorders' and their manifestations, we have to recognize that despite some common themes, each person and situation is unique and will require creativity and collaboration.

While one of the strengths of the restorative justice conferencing model we describe in this book is its structure and simplicity, it is worth noting again that some situations will require additional skills and expertise. Conferences involving people with complex needs require, at every stage of the process, sensitivity to and comfort with the needs and struggles faced by those participants. It is essential that the person facilitating a conference is the best person for that role. This means that they are experienced and adept at working with people like those in their conference, or that they have with them a support person who has those skills and with whom the facilitator can consult in preparing for and conducting a conference.

At this point in time, the way that we are going about making inclusion possible in Toronto, is through the development of the Toronto Restorative Justice Network. While we have found this to be an effective and efficient way to make conferencing available to and inclusive of people with complex needs, we don't imagine that it is the only way. This was, for us, a fairly intuitive response that reflects the relative wealth of community resources often found in large urban environments, as well as our history of using the network model to address other service needs in the community. Other communities will no doubt find creative ways of ensuring inclusion that are suited to their contexts.

Finally, I want to emphasize that restorative justice conferencing is not a panacea or a 'technique' with universal applications. Although the values that characterize restorative practices, including conferences and circles, should inform and influence all of our communities and institutions, not all situations are going to lend themselves to the use of conferences. It is important for facilitators to be clear about those situations in which they believe a conference does not meet the threshold I mentioned earlier in this chapter. Conferences are intended to repair harm, not add to it, and they should not be conducted until all of the participants are prepared and have some confidence about what they can contribute and take away from the experience.[12] Nothing, not even a looming court date, should cause us to rush participants into or through the process. It must reflect their pace and honour their needs and wishes. It is, after all, incumbent upon us to ensure that we earn and keep the trust bestowed upon us as facilitators by the communities we are helping to repair.

(Footnotes)

[1] The distinction that I make between conferences and circles is largely one of formality. Although both are informed by the same values and beliefs about community, harm and healing, conferences are more formal and will involve more preparation. A circle is a sort of mini-conference that may be more spontaneous and may be done in situations where the participants are already present, known to each other, and familiar with restorative practices. These might be done in a school program as a way of 'processing' and resolving an incident soon after it happened.

[2] The Griffin Centre is a children's mental health centre in Toronto that specializes in working with dually diagnosed youth, by which we mean youth who have an intellectual or developmental disability along with mental health problems.

[3] We are using this term as a sort of umbrella for a range of struggles, including developmental disabilities and disorders, mental health concerns and significant learning/communication disorders.

[4] These are trading cards that people (mostly children) collect and use to play a fantasy game.

[5] Although some of what is discussed herein may apply to people with more pronounced intellectual disabilities, we refer primarily to experiences derived from working with people who have what is termed a

"mild" disability.

[6] Although not ideal, it is even possible to do a circle in segments so as to permit a restless participant the opportunity to take short breaks. It is important if doing a conference in this way, however, to ensure that there is a clear structure so that breaks are at predictable intervals rather than happening spontaneously (thus potentially cutting someone off in mid-sentence).

[7] The existence of both an intellectual disability and concurrent mental health struggles.

[8] For further information about the Toronto Restorative Justice Network or the network model, please call the Griffin Centre in Toronto at 416-222-1153 and ask for the TRJN Coordinator.

[9] At present, The Toronto Restorative Justice Network is mandated to respond to situations in which the transgressor is a youth between the ages of 12 and 17. We do, however, sometimes get involved in situations with young adults, and where one of the other participants is a youth with complex needs.

[10] By the end of the pilot phase of the TRJN project we had trained approximately 90 workers across the City of Toronto.

[11] This acronym stands for Lesbian, Gay, Bisexual, Transexual/Transvestite, Two-Spirited.

[12] In the TRJN, for example, we have yet to develop best practice guidelines for conducting conferences for situations where there has been sexual abuse. Until those guidelines have been developed, and until we have properly trained facilitators who also have extensive experience in working with those who have been affected by or perpetrated sexual abuse, we will refrain from doing so.

#82
"Honouring Woman"

With sacred pipe in hand she prays. She prays for her community. She calls upon the people dancing. Teach us to dance with the grass, touching our mother, the earth. It is from her that her daughters continue to nourish life of all and strengthen the minds and hearts of all.

The Youth Criminal Justice Act (YCJA) (Ontario)

Legislative Structure

We decided to insert the actual Ontario legislation here because if we simply said 'look it up', most of you would not manage to make the time, let alone actually reading it. We recognize that this is the **Ontario legislation**. However, it is real legislation and it can be used as a lever to create new options for youth. It is important. It turns out that most of the time, we can do a many things which common mythology sugests, "you can't". Have a look at this legislation so you can see what it actually says and thus imagine what you can do. Read it now!

(Note: Clearly you need to read the appropriate legislation for your jurisdiction, but if there is a Restorative Justice component, it will likely have some similarities. If there isn't, perhaps this model can be used to begin a new legislative option.)

Restorative Justice Philosophy Reflected and Reinforced in the Youth Criminal Justice Act

The individual if left alone from birth would remain primitive and beastlike in thoughts and feelings to a degree that we can hardly conceive. The individual is what he is and has significance that he has not so much in virtue of his individuality, but rather as a member of the great human community, which directs his material and spiritual existence from the cradle to the grave.
Albert Einstein

Implications

There is a theme that weaves throughout the Youth Criminal Justice Act (YCJA), it is community. The concept of community is found no less than 34 times in the legislation. The concept of community is further reinforced an additional 22 times by way of the terms: society, public, rehabilitation, and reintegration. Community is at the core of restorative justice. As mentioned, community is not just a place - it is a process, a process of finding our place in the world. Community is about relationships. The healthier the relationships, the healthier the community, and thus the healthier the society. The sections of the legislation which reflect community in the (YCJA) are highlighted in this section of the book.

Statutes of Canada

CHAPTER 1

An Act in respect of criminal justice for young persons and to amend and repeal other Acts

WHEREAS members of society share a responsibility to address the developmental challenges and the needs of young persons and to guide them into adulthood;

WHEREAS communities, families, parents and others concerned with the development of young persons should, through multi-disciplinary approaches, take reasonable steps to prevent youth crime by addressing its underlying causes, to respond to the needs of young persons, and to provide guidance and support to those at risk of committing crimes;

WHEREAS information about youth justice, youth crime and the effectiveness of measures taken to address youth crime should be publicly available;

WHEREAS Canada is a party to the United Nations Convention on the Rights of the Child and recognizes that young persons have rights and freedoms, including those stated in the *Canadian Charter of Rights and Freedoms* and the *Canadian Bill of Rights*, and have special guarantees of their rights and freedoms;

AND WHEREAS Canadian society should have a youth criminal justice system that commands respect, takes into account the interests of victims, fosters responsibility and ensures accountability through meaningful consequences and effective ***rehabilitation and reintegration***, and that reserves its most serious intervention for the most serious crimes and ***reduces the over-reliance on incarceration for non-violent young persons;***

NOW, THEREFORE, Her Majesty, by and with the advice and consent of the Senate and House of Commons of Canada, enacts as follows:

Implications

The fundamental theme that is represented in the opening preamble to the Youth Criminal Justice Act is community (see italicized above). The implication here is that no longer will one institution (such as the police, the courts, the correctional system) have exclusive domain in dealing with youth who come into conflict with the law. Clearly, the YCJA states that all members of society must be involved in the guidance of our young people, particularly when they are in a state of conflict.

The challenge this philosophy puts before us is to discover just how we all are, in very practical ways, enabled and enlisted to assist our young people in times of crisis, conflict and disconnection from community. In addition, we need to be clear who will determine what community means. And just how will the links and relationships be created between exitsting agencies, institutions and communities?

DECLARATION OF PRINCIPLE

3. (1) The following principles apply in this Act:

(*a*) the youth criminal justice system is intended to

(i) prevent crime by addressing the circumstances underlying a young person's offending behaviour,

(ii) ***rehabilitate young persons who commit offences and reintegrate them into society, and***

(iii) ensure that a young person is subject to meaningful consequences for his or her offence

in order to promote the long-term ***protection of the public;***

(*b*) the criminal justice system for young persons must be separate from that of adults and emphasize the following:

(i) ***rehabilitation and reintegration,***

(ii) fair and proportionate accountability that is consistent with the greater dependency of young persons and their reduced level of maturity,

Policy for Canada with respect to young persons

(iii) enhanced procedural protection to ensure that young persons are treated fairly and that their rights, including their right to privacy, are protected,

(iv) timely intervention that reinforces the link between the offending behaviour and its consequences, and

(v) the promptness and speed with which persons responsible for enforcing this Act must act, given young persons' perception of time;

(*c*) within the limits of fair and proportionate accountability, the measures taken against young persons who commit offences should

(i) ***reinforce respect for societal values,***

(ii) ***encourage the repair of harm done to victims and the community,***

(iii) be meaningful for the individual young person given his or her needs and level of development and, where appropriate, involve the parents, the extended family, ***the community and social or other agencies in the young person's rehabilitation and reintegration,*** and

(iv) respect gender, ethnic, cultural and linguistic differences and respond to the needs of aboriginal young persons and of young persons with special requirements; and

(d) special considerations applyspecial considerations apply in respect of proceedings against young persons and, in particular,

(i) young persons have rights and freedoms in their own right, such as a right to be heard in the course of and to participate in the processes, other than the decision to prosecute, that lead to decisions that affect them, and young persons have special guarantees of their rights and freedoms,

(ii) victims should be treated with courtesy, compassion and respect for their dignity and privacy and should suffer the minimum degree of inconvenience as a result of their involvement with the youth criminal justice system,

(iii) victims should be provided with information about the proceedings and given an opportunity to participate and be heard, and

(iv) parents should be informed of measures or proceedings involving their children and encouraged to support them in addressing their offending behaviour.

2) This Act shall be liberally construed so as to ensure that young persons are dealt with in accordance with the principles set out in subsection (1).

Act to be liberally construed

Implications

The notion of rehabilitation and reintegration is referred to in 3 different sections of the Declaration of Principles. The central questions this reference generates are: rehabilitation of what? And reintegration to where? Often, all too often for people who are in conflict nor is it a matter of rehabilitation as much as it is of habilitation; it is not a matter of reintegration as much as it is a matter of integration. This is to say that the skills which agencies seek to rehabilitate assume the young person had the skills and somehow they are no longer using these skills and all that needs to be done now is return to the missing skill set. Furthermore, many of the young people have never known integration in the first place. Rather their story is one of isolation and disintegration on a great many levels.

The challenge, given this reality, is for all of us to pause and reflect on how we create ways to include integration and habilitation as the initial phase on working with young people. To reflect on this small step is to see the potential and the capacity of this legislation as being a catalyst of true social transformation of our criminal and social justice systems. At the core of this challenge is to find ways for community members to be integrated into the formal structures with a focus on young people staying in community not in custody.

PART I

EXTRAJUDICIAL MEASURES

Principles and Objectives
4. The following principles apply in this Part in addition to the principles set out in section 3:

(*a*) **extrajudicial measures are often the most appropriate and effective way to address youth crime**;

(*b*) extrajudicial measures allow for effective and timely interventions focused on correcting offending behaviour;

Declaration of principles

(*c*) extrajudicial measures are presumed to be adequate to hold a young person accountable for his or her offending behaviour if the young person has committed a non-violent offence and has not previously been found guilty of an offence; and

(*d*) extrajudicial measures should be used if they are adequate to hold a young person accountable for his or her offending behaviour and, if the use of extrajudicial measures is consistent with the principles set out in this section, nothing in this Act precludes their use in respect of a young person who

(i) has previously been dealt with by the use of extrajudicial measures, or

(ii) has previously been found guilty of an offence.

Implications

This section along with section 5, is stating explicitly that keeping young people away from the criminal justice systems is far more effective than bringing them into the system. In fact by the end of the tenure of the Young Offenders Act (YOA), Canada had the highest incarceration rate of young people in the world. Furthermore, it was agreed that the longer a young person remained in custody the greater the likelihood of that person re-offending. So what we now have is legislation, which mandates ways to reinforce community-building process; ways that are outside the formal boundaries of the criminal justice system and keep the young person in a place of community. Again it is in community where a person will develop the skills and experience the strength of integration and connection, rather than the experience of isolation and debilitation that comes from custody.

5. Extrajudicial measures should be designed to

(*a*) provide an effective and timely response to offending behaviour **outside the bounds of judicial measures;**

(*b*) encourage young persons to acknowledge and **repair the harm caused to the victim and the community;**

(*c*) **encourage families of young persons — including extended families where appropriate — and the community to become involved in the design and implementation of those measures;**

(*d*) provide an opportunity for victims to participate in decisions related to the measures selected and to receive reparation; and (*e*) respect the rights and freedoms of young persons and be proportionate to the seriousness of the offence.

Warnings, cautions and referrals

6. (1) A police officer shall, before starting judicial proceedings or taking any other measures under this Act against a young person alleged to have committed an offence, consider whether it would be sufficient, having regard to the principles set out in section 4, to take no further action, warn the young person, administer a caution, if a program has been established under section 7, or, with the consent of the young person, refer the young person to a program or *agency in the community that may assist the young person not to commit offences*.

Saving

(2) The failure of a police officer to consider the options set out in subsection (1) does not invalidate any subsequent charges against the young person for the offence.

Implications

For the first time there is a legislative mandate for the police to actively explore ways, alternatives to pursuing formal criminal charges of the young person. And in each of these ways there will be the concept of community, for at the core of community are relationships. This process creates the opportunity for restorative justice practices to become an integral part of the overall process by way of bringing the community members closer to the justice system be it through formal programming, mentoring, facilitating circles to name just three areas. The idea of community involvement by way of having the young person remain outside of the formal criminal justice system is further reinforced in the subsequent sections 7,8,9 by way of the attorney general supporting programs that have a community focus and allowing the young person to remain outside the formal criminal justice system.

Perhaps the most significant implication of this section is the implied invitation for justice workers such as the police, probation/parole officers, open/secure custody staff, mental health practitioners, to explore ways to integrate the community-building, restorative justice philosophy and skill sets within their existing roles and responsibilities.

Police cautions

7. The Attorney General, or any other minister designated by the lieutenant governor of a province, may establish a program authorizing the police to administer cautions to young persons instead of starting judicial proceedings under this Act.

Crown cautions

8. The Attorney General may establish a program authorizing prosecutors to administer cautions to young persons instead of starting or continuing judicial proceedings under this Act.

Evidence of measures is inadmissible

9. Evidence that a young person has received a warning, caution or referral mentioned in section 6, 7 or 8 or that a police officer has taken no further action in respect of an offence, and evidence of the offence, is inadmissible for the purpose of proving prior offending behaviour in any proceedings before a youth justice court in respect of the young person.

Extrajudicial Sanctions

Extrajudicial sanctions

10. (1) An extrajudicial sanction may be used to deal with a young person alleged to have committed an offence only if the young person cannot be adequately dealt with by a warning, caution or referral mentioned in section 6, 7 or 8 because of the seriousness of the offence, the nature and number of previous offences committed by the young person or any other aggravating circumstances.

Conditions   (2) An extrajudicial sanction may be used only if

(a) ***it is part of a program of sanctions that may be authorized by the Attorney General or authorized by a person, or a member of a class of persons, designated by the lieutenant governor in council of the province;***

(b) ***the person who is considering whether to use the extrajudicial sanction is satisfied that it would be appropriate, having regard to the needs of the young person and the interests of society;***

(c) the young person, having been informed of the extrajudicial sanction, fully and freely consents to be subject to it;

(d) the young person has, before consenting to be subject to the extrajudicial sanction, been advised of his or her right to be represented by counsel and been given a reasonable opportunity to consult with counsel;

(e) ***the young person accepts responsibility for the act or omission that forms the basis of the offence that he or she is alleged to have committed***;

(f) there is, in the opinion of the Attorney General, sufficient evidence to proceed with the prosecution of the offence; and

(g) the prosecution of the offence is not in any way barred at law.

Restriction on use (3) An extrajudicial sanction may not be used in respect of a young person who

(a) denies participation or involvement in the commission of the offence; or

(b) expresses the wish to have the charge dealt with by a youth justice court.

Admissions not admissible in evidence   (4) Any admission, confession or statement accepting responsibility for a given act or omission that is made by a young person as a condition of being dealt with by an extrajudicial sanction is inadmissible in evidence against any young person in civil or criminal proceedings.

No bar to judicial proceedings   (5) The use of an extrajudicial sanction in respect of a young person alleged to have committed an offence is not a bar to judicial proceedings under this Act, but if a charge is laid against the young person in respect of the offence,

(a) ***the youth justice court shall dismiss the charge if it is satisfied on a balance of probabilities that the young person has totally complied with the terms and conditions of the extrajudicial sanction; and***

(b) ***the youth justice court may dismiss the charge if it is satisfied on a balance of probabilities that the young person has partially complied with the terms and conditions of the extrajudicial sanction and if, in the opinion of the court, prosecution of the charge would be unfair having regard to the circumstances and the young person's performance with respect to the extrajudicial sanction.***

Laying of
information, etc.

(6) Subject to subsection (5) and section 24 (private prosecutions only with consent of Attorney General), nothing in this section shall be construed as preventing any person from laying an information or indictment, obtaining the issue or confirmation of any process or proceeding with the prosecution of any offence in accordance with law.

Implications

Section 10 above, is one step up in more formal intervention by the criminal justice system, but again it is a process which is reinforcing the idea of keeping the young person in community, rather than drawing the person further into the criminal justice process.

Youth Justice
Committees

Youth justice
committees

18. *(1) The Attorney General of Canada or a province or any other minister that the lieutenant governor in council of the province may designate may establish one or more committees of citizens, to be known as youth justice committees, to assist in any aspect of the administration of this Act or in any programs or services for young persons.*

Role of
committee

(2) The functions of a youth justice committee may include the following:

(*a*) in the case of a young person alleged to have committed an offence,

(i) *giving advice on the appropriate extrajudicial measure to be used in respect of the young person*

(ii) supporting any victim of the alleged offence by soliciting his or her concerns and facilitating the reconciliation of the victim and the young person,

(iii) ensuring that community support is available to the young person by arranging for the use of services from within the community, and enlisting members of the community to provide short-term mentoring and supervision, and

(iv) when the young person is also being dealt with by a child protection agency or a community group, helping to coordinate the interaction of the agency or group with the youth criminal justice system;

(b) advising the federal and provincial governments on whether the provisions of this Act that grant rights to young persons, or provide for the protection of young persons, are being complied with;

(c) advising the federal and provincial governments on policies and procedures related to the youth criminal justice system;

(d) providing information to the public in respect of this Act and the youth criminal justice system;

(*e*) *acting as a conference; and*

(f) any other functions assigned by the person who establishes the committee

Conferences

Conferences may
be convened

19. (1) A youth justice court judge, the provincial director, a police officer, a justice of the peace, a prosecutor or a youth worker may convene or cause to be convened a conference for the purpose of making a decision required to be made under this Act.

Mandate of a
conference

(2) The mandate of a conference may be, among other things, to give advice on appropriate extrajudicial measures, conditions for judicial interim release, sentences, including the review of sentences, and reintegration plans.

Rules for conferences	(3) The Attorney General or any other minister designated by the lieutenant governor in council of a province may establish rules for the convening and conducting of conferences other than conferences convened or caused to be convened by a youth justice court judge or a justice of the peace.
Rules to apply	(4) In provinces where rules are established under subsection (3), the conferences to which those rules apply must be convened and conducted in accordance with those rules.

Implications

The two sections (18-19) above, are on the scale of organizational transformation and social transformation. The legislation is saying in these two sections that citizens and citizen committees are to be an essential part of the reintegration plans of the young person who has come into conflict with the law. Once again the challenge here will be to find way of creating committees, determining who constitutes a committee, what is the full mandate of the citizen committee, to what extent will they be able to impact on matters of policy and practices? There will need to be clarity on what is meant by conference. There are a variety of conference processes which range from sentencing circles to healing circles and included restorative justice circles as well as family group conferencing. The challenge is exciting because it demands of us all to engage in ways that can truly nurture positive transformation for everyone involved.

JUDICIAL MEASURES

Consent to Prosecute

Pre-charge screening	**23.** (1) The Attorney General may establish *a program of pre-charge screening* that sets out the circumstances in which the consent of the Attorney General must be obtained before a young person is charged with an offence.
Pre-charge screening program	(2) Any *program of pre-charge screening of young persons* that is established under an Act of the legislature of a province or by a directive of a provincial government, and that is in place before the coming into force of this section, is deemed to be a program of pre-charge screening for the purposes of subsection (1).

Implications

To have a pre-charge screening process further reinforces the need to explore the potential to have the young person stay, where and when appropriate, integrated within community rather than excluded from community. Furthermore, these two sections reinforce sections 4, 6 by providing the impetus for professionals to develop skills in the restorative justice community-building framework. These skill sets would be one major step towards a potential transformation of the existing roles for all justice professionals.

PART 4

SENTENCING

Purpose and Principles

Purpose | **38.** (1) The purpose of sentencing under section 42 (youth sentences) is to hold a young person accountable for an offence through the imposition of just sanctions that have meaningful consequences for the young person and that promote his or her *rehabilitation and reintegration into society, thereby contributing to the long-term protection of the public.*

Sentencing principles | (2) A youth justice court that imposes a youth sentence on a young person shall determine the sentence in accordance with the principles set out in section 3 and the following principles:

(*a*) the sentence must not result in a punishment that is greater than the punishment that would be appropriate for an adult who has been convicted of the same offence committed in similar circumstances;

(*b*) the sentence must be similar to the sentences imposed in the region on similar young persons found guilty of the same offence committed in similar circumstances;

(*c*) *the sentence must be proportionate to the seriousness of the offence and the degree of responsibility of the young person for that offence;*

(*d*) all available sanctions other than custody that are reasonable in the circumstances should be considered for all young persons, with particular attention to the circumstances of aboriginal young persons; and

(*e*) subject to paragraph (*c*), the sentence must

(i) be the least restrictive sentence that is capable of achieving the purpose set out in subsection (1),

(ii*) be the one that is most likely to rehabilitate the young person and reintegrate him or her into society, and*

(*iii) promote a sense of the responsibility in the young person, and an acknowledgment of the harm done to victims and the community.*

Factors to be considered

(3) In determining a youth sentence, the youth justice court shall take into account

(*a*) the degree of participation by the young person in the commission of the offence;

(*b*) the harm done to victims and whether it was intentional or reasonably foreseeable;

(*c*) **any reparation made by the young person to the victim or the community**;

(*d*) the time spent in detention by the young person as a result of the offence;

(*e*) the previous findings of guilt of the young person; and

(*f*) any other aggravating and mitigating circumstances related to the young person or the offence that are relevant to the purpose and principles set out in this section.

Implications

The sentencing principles above are a reflection of the Declaration of Principles in section 3 or the YCJA. Again the theme reflected here is community, by way of repairing harm done through the process of rehabilitation and reintegration. It is important to see that the focus on repairing harm done is now including the concept of community. This phrasing is an explicit illustration of the philosophy of restorative justice, which as stated earlier has at its very core the belief in nurturing community.

Youth Sentences

Recommendation of conference

41. When a youth justice court finds a young person guilty of an offence, the court may convene or cause to be convened a conference under section 19 for recommendations to the court on an appropriate youth sentence.

Implications

This section (41) represents the reinforcement of the entire conferencing process, which is central to the practice of restorative justice models.

Considerations as to youth sentence

42. (1) A youth justice court shall, before imposing a youth sentence, consider any recommendations submitted under section 41, any pre-sentence report, any representations made by the parties to the proceedings or their counsel or agents and by the parents of the young person, and any other relevant information before the court.

Youth sentence

(2) When a youth justice court finds a young person guilty of an offence and is imposing a youth sentence, the court shall, subject to this section, impose any one of the following sanctions or any number of them that are not inconsistent with each other and, if the offence is first degree murder or second degree murder within the meaning of section 231 of the *Criminal Code*, the court shall impose a sanction set out in paragraph (*q*) or subparagraph (*r*)(ii) or (iii) and may impose any other of the sanctions set out in this subsection that the court considers appropriate:

(*a*) reprimand the young person;

(*b*) by order direct that the young person be discharged absolutely, if the court considers it to be in the best interests of the young person and not contrary to the public interest;

(*c*) by order direct that the young person be discharged on any conditions that the court considers appropriate and may require the young person to report to and be supervised by the provincial director;

(*d*) impose on the young person a fine not exceeding $1,000 to be paid at the time and on the terms that the court may fix;

(*e*) order the young person to pay to any other person at the times and on the terms that the court may fix an amount by way of compensation for loss of or damage to property or for loss of income or support, or an amount for, in the Province of Quebec, pre-trial pecuniary loss or, in any other province, special damages, for personal injury arising from the commission of the offence if the value is readily ascertainable, but no order shall be made for other damages in the Province of Quebec or for general damages in any other province;

(*f*) order the young person to make restitution to any other person of any property obtained by the young person as a result of the commission of the offence within the time that the court may fix, if the property is owned by the other person or was, at the time of the offence, in his or her lawful possession;

(*g*) if property obtained as a result of the commission of the offence has been sold to an innocent purchaser, where restitution of the property to its owner or any other person has been made or ordered, order the young person to pay the purchaser, at the time and on the terms that the court may fix, an amount not exceeding the amount paid by the purchaser for the property;

(*h*) subject to section 54, order the young person to compensate any person in kind or by way of personal services at the time and on the terms that the court may fix for any loss, damage or injury suffered by that person in respect of which an order may be made under paragraph (*e*) or (*g*);

Agreement of provincial director

(3) A youth justice court may make an order under paragraph (2)(*l*) or (*m*) only if the provincial director has determined that a program to enforce the order is available.

Youth justice court statement

(4) When the youth justice court makes a custody and supervision order with respect to a young person under paragraph (2)(*n*), the court shall state the following with respect to that order:

You are ordered to serve (*state the number of days or months to be served*) in custody, to be followed by (*state one-half of the number of days or months stated above*) **to be served under supervision in the community subject to conditions.**

If you breach any of the conditions while you are under supervision in the community, you may be brought back into custody and required to serve the rest of the second period in custody as well.

You should also be aware that, under other provisions of the *Youth Criminal Justice Act,* a court could require you to serve the second period in custody as well.

The periods in custody and under supervision in the community may be changed if you are or become subject to another sentence.

Deferred custody and supervision order

(5) The court may make a deferred custody and supervision order under paragraph (2)(*p*) if

(*a*) the young person is found guilty of an offence that is not a serious violent offence; and

(*b*) it is consistent with the purpose and principles set out in section 38 and the restrictions on custody set out in section 39.

Application of sections 106 to 109

(6) Sections 106 to 109 (suspension of conditional supervision) apply to a breach of a deferred custody and supervision order made under paragraph (2)(*p*) as if the breach were a breach of an order for conditional supervision made under subsection 105(1) and, for the purposes of sections 106 to 109, supervision under a deferred custody and supervision order is deemed to be conditional supervision.

Intensive rehabilitative custody and supervision order

(7) A youth justice court may make an ***intensive rehabilitative custody and supervision*** order under paragraph (2)(*r*) in respect of a young person only if

(*a*) either

(i) the young person has been found guilty of an offence under one of the following provisions of the *Criminal Code,* namely, section 231 or 235 (first degree murder or second degree murder within the meaning of section 231), section 239 (attempt to commit murder), section 232, 234 or 236 (manslaughter), or section 273 (aggravated sexual assault), or

(ii) the young person has been found guilty of a serious violent offence for which an adult is liable to imprisonment for a term of more than two years, and the young person had previously been found guilty at least twice of a serious violent offence;

(*b*) the young person is suffering from a mental illness or disorder, a psychological disorder or an emotional disturbance;

(*c*) ***a plan of treatment and intensive supervision*** has been developed for the young person, and there are reasonable grounds to believe that the plan might reduce the risk of the young person repeating the offence or committing a serious violent offence; and

(*d*) the provincial director has determined tha***t an intensive rehabilitative custody and supervision program*** is available and that the young person's participation in the program is appropriate.

Safeguard of rights

(8) Nothing in this section abrogates or derogates from the rights of a young person regarding consent to physical or mental health treatment or care.

Determination by court

(9) On application of the Attorney General after a young person is found guilty of an offence, and after giving both parties an opportunity to be heard, the youth justice court may make a judicial determination that the offence is a serious violent offence and endorse the information or indictment accordingly.

Appeals

(10) For the purposes of an appeal in accordance with section 37, a determination under subsection (9) is part of the sentence.

Inconsistency

(11) An order may not be made under paragraphs (2)(*k*) to (*m*) in respect of an offence for which a conditional discharge has been granted under paragraph (2)(*c*).

Coming into force of youth sentence

(12) A youth sentence or any part of it comes into force on the date on which it is imposed or on any later date that the youth justice court specifies.

Consecutive youth sentences

(13) Subject to subsections (15) and (16), a youth justice court that sentences a young person may direct that a sentence imposed on the young person under paragraph (2)(*n*), (*o*), (*q*) or (*r*) be served consecutively if the young person

(*a*) is sentenced while under sentence for an offence under any of those paragraphs; or

(*b*) is found guilty of more than one offence under any of those paragraphs.

Duration of youth sentence for a single offence

(14) No youth sentence, other than an order made under paragraph (2)(*j*), (*n*), (*o*), (*q*) or (*r*), shall continue in force for more than two years. If the youth sentence comprises more than one sanction imposed at the same time in respect of the same offence, the combined duration of the sanctions shall not exceed two years, unless the sentence includes a sanction under paragraph (2)(*j*), (*n*), (*o*), (*q*) or (*r*) that exceeds two years.

Duration of youth sentence for different offences

(15) Subject to subsection (16), if more than one youth sentence is imposed under this section in respect of a young person with respect to different offences, the continuous combined duration of those youth sentences shall not exceed three years, except if one of the offences is first degree murder or second degree murder within the meaning of section 231 of the *Criminal Code*, in which case the continuous combined duration of those youth sentences shall not exceed ten years in the case of first degree murder, or seven years in the case of second degree murder.

Duration of youth sentences made at different times

(16) If a youth sentence is imposed in respect of an offence committed by a young person after the commencement of, but before the completion of, any youth sentences imposed on the young person,

(*a*) the duration of the sentence imposed in respect of the subsequent offence shall be determined in accordance with subsections (14) and (15);

(*b*) the sentence may be served consecutively to the sentences imposed in respect of the previous offences; and

(*c*) the combined duration of all the sentences may exceed three years and, if the offence is, or one of the previous offences was,

(i) first degree murder within the meaning of section 231 of the *Criminal Code*, the continuous combined duration of the youth sentences may exceed ten years, or

(ii) second degree murder within the meaning of section 231 of the *Criminal Code*, the continuous combined duration of the youth sentences may exceed seven years.

Sentence continues when adult	(17) Subject to sections 89, 92 and 93 (provisions related to placement in adult facilities) of this Act and section 743.5 (transfer of jurisdiction) of the *Criminal Code*, a youth sentence imposed on a young person continues in effect in accordance with its terms after the young person becomes an adult.
Supervision when additional youth sentence extends the period in custody	**45.** (1) If a young person has begun to serve a portion of a youth sentence in the community subject to conditions under paragraph 42(2)(*n*) or under conditional supervision under paragraph 42(2)(*o*), (*q*) or (*r*) at the time an additional youth sentence is imposed under one of those paragraphs, and, as a result of the application of section 44, the custodial portion of the young person's youth sentence ends on a day that is later than the day on which the young person received the additional youth sentence, the serving of a portion of the youth sentence under supervision in the community subject to conditions or under conditional supervision shall become inoperative and the young person shall be committed to custody under paragraph 102(1)(*b*) or 106(*b*) until the end of the extended portion of the youth sentence to be served in custody.
Supervision when additional youth sentence does not extend the period in custody	(2) If a youth sentence has been imposed under paragraph 42(2)(*n*), (*o*), (*q*) or (*r*) on a young person who is under supervision in the community subject to conditions under paragraph 42(2)(*n*) or under conditional supervision under paragraph 42(2)(*o*), (*q*) or (*r*), and the additional youth sentence would not modify the expiry date of the youth sentence that the young person was serving at the time the additional youth sentence was imposed, the young person may be remanded to the youth custody facility that the provincial director considers appropriate. The provincial director shall review the case and, no later than forty-eight hours after the remand of the young person, shall either refer the case to the youth justice court for a review under section 103 or 109 or release the young person to continue the supervision in the community or the conditional supervision.
Supervision when youth sentence additional to supervision	(3) If a youth sentence has been imposed under paragraph 42(2)(*n*), (*o*), (*q*) or (*r*) on a young person who is under conditional supervision under paragraph 94(19)(*b*) or subsection 96(5), the young person shall be remanded to the youth custody facility that the provincial director considers appropriate. The provincial director shall review the case and, no later than forty-eight hours after the remand of the young person, shall either refer the case to the youth justice court for a review under section 103 or 109 or release the young person to continue the conditional supervision

Implications

While section 42 addresses all of the sentencing options of the justice system including custody, it is important to note that the most common disposition invoked is probation and that probation is a community disposition. Further there is a growing need and request by probation officers to be develop ties and relationships with community members on many levels ranging from volunteer probation officers to community based programming.

PART 5

CUSTODY AND SUPERVISION

Purpose

83. (1) The purpose of the youth custody and supervision system is to contribute to the protection of society by

(*a*) carrying out sentences imposed by courts through the safe, fair and humane custody and supervision of young persons; and

(*b*) **assisting young persons to be rehabilitated and reintegrated into the community as law-abiding citizens, by providing effective programs to young persons in custody and while under supervision in the community**.

Principles to be used

(2*) In addition to the principles set out in section 3, the following principles are to be used in achieving that purpose:*

(a) that the least restrictive measures consistent with the protection of the public, of personnel working with young persons and of young persons be used;

(*b*) that young persons sentenced to custody retain the rights of other young persons, except the rights that are necessarily removed or restricted as a consequence of a sentence under this Act or another Act of Parliament;

(*c) that the youth custody and supervision system facilitate the involvement of the families of young persons and members of the public*;

(*d*) that custody and supervision decisions be made in a forthright, fair and timely manner, and that young persons have access to an effective review procedure; and

(*e*) that placements of young persons where they are treated as adults not disadvantage them with respect to their eligibility for and conditions of release.

Levels of custody

85. (1) In the youth custody and supervision system in each province there must be at least two levels of custody for young persons distinguished by the degree of restraint of the young persons in them.

Designation of youth custody facilities

(2) Every youth custody facility in a province that contains one or more levels of custody shall be designated by

(*a*) in the case of a youth custody facility with only one level of custody, being the level of custody with the least degree of restraint of the young persons in it, the lieutenant governor in council or his or her delegate; and

(*b*) in any other case, the lieutenant governor in council.

Provincial director to specify custody level - committal to custody

(3) The provincial director shall, when a young person is committed to custody under paragraph 42(2)(*n*), (*o*), (*q*) or (*r*) or an order is made under subsection 98(3), paragraph 103(2)(*b*), subsection 104(1) or paragraph 109(2)(*b*), determine the level of custody appropriate for the young person, after having taken into account the factors set out in subsection (5).

Provincial director to specify custody level - transfer

(4) The provincial director may determine a different level of custody for the young person when the provincial director is satisfied that the needs of the young person and the interests of society would be better served by doing so, after having taken into account the factors set out in subsection (5).

Factors

(5) The factors referred to in subsections (3) and (4) are

(*a*) that the appropriate level of custody for the young person is the one that is the least restrictive to the young person, having regard to

(i) the seriousness of the offence in respect of which the young person was committed to custody and the circumstances in which that offence was committed,

(ii) the needs and circumstances of the young person, including proximity to family, school, employment and support services,

(iii) the safety of other young persons in custody, and

(iv) the interests of society;

(*b*) that the level of custody should allow for the best possible match of programs to the young person's needs and behaviour, having regard to the findings of any assessment in respect of the young person; and

(*c*) the likelihood of escape.

Placement and
transfer at appropriate
level

(6) After the provincial director has determined the appropriate level of custody for the young person under subsection (3) or (4), the young person shall be placed in the youth custody facility that contains that level of custody specified by the provincial director.

Notice

(7) The provincial director shall cause a notice in writing of a determination under subsection (3) or (4) to be given to the young person and a parent of the young person and set out in that notice the reasons for it.

Implications

It is critical to realize that very, very few people are held in custody indefinitely. Only those who are assessed as dangerous offenders are in custody indefinitely. So in essence everyone who is sentenced to a period of custody will some day be released back into society. Therefore, the question remains, how do we want these people to be when they return to society? What will allow them to return and maintain public safety and community well-being?

Youth worker

90. (1) When a youth sentence is imposed committing a young person to custody, the provincial director of the province in which the young person received the youth sentence and was placed in custody shall, without delay, designate a youth worker to work with the young person to plan for his or her reintegration into the community, including the preparation and implementation of a reintegration plan that sets out the most effective programs for the young person in order to maximize his or her chances for reintegration into the community.

Role of youth worker
when young person in
the community

(2) When a portion of a young person's youth sentence is served in the community in accordance with section 97 or 105, the youth worker shall supervise the young person, continue to provide support to the young person and assist the young person to respect the conditions to which he or she is subject, and help the young person in the implementation of the reintegration plan.

Reintegration leave	91. (1) The provincial director of a province may, subject to any terms or conditions that he or she considers desirable, authorize, for a young person committed to a youth custody facility in the province further to an order under paragraph 76(1)(a) (placement when subject to adult sentence) or a youth sentence imposed under paragraph 42(2)(n), (o), (q) or (r),

(a) a reintegration leave from the youth custody facility for a period not exceeding thirty days if, in the opinion of the provincial director, it is necessary or desirable that the young person be absent, with or without escort, for medical, compassionate or humanitarian reasons or for the purpose of rehabilitating the young person or reintegrating the young person into the community; or

(b) that the young person be released from the youth custody facility on the days and during the hours that the provincial director specifies in order that the young person may

(i) attend school or any other educational or training institution,

(ii) obtain or continue employment or perform domestic or other duties required by the young person's family,

(iii) participate in a program specified by the provincial director that, in the provincial director's opinion, will enable the young person to better carry out employment or improve his or her education or training, or

(iv) attend an out-patient treatment program or other program that provides services that are suitable to addressing the young person's needs.

Renewal of reintegration leave	(2) A reintegration leave authorized under paragraph (1)(a) may be renewed by the provincial director for one or more thirty-day periods on reassessment of the case.
Revocation of authorization	(3) The provincial director of a province may, at any time, revoke an authorization made under subsection (1).
Arrest and return to custody	(4) If the provincial director revokes an authorization under subsection (3) or if a young person fails to comply with any term or condition of a reintegration leave or a release from custody under this section, the young person may be arrested without warrant and returned to custody.

Implications

Under the previous legislation one of the concerns was that youth were "falling through the cracks", in so far that upon their release from custody they returned to their old way of behaviour. In essence there was no strategic plan or process in place and no one there for them upon their release. Now with the YCJA, there is a designated person (youth worker) who is there prior to and during the reintegration of the young person. Once again the focus here is on community. The youth worker is someone who is central to the process of building relationships, which will support the young person's return to society.

The youth worker is also the one who works with young people who are not in custody but are under community supervision by way of probation dispositions. And again this process takes place within the model and philosophy of building community for the young person.

> **96.** (1*) When a young person is held in custody pursuant to a youth sentence under paragraph 42(2)(n), (o), (q) or (r), the provincial director may, if satisfied that the needs of the young person and the interests of society would be better served by doing so, make a recommendation to the youth justice court that the young person be released from custody and placed under conditional supervision*.

Notice

(2) If the provincial director makes a recommendation, the provincial director shall cause a notice to be given in writing that includes the reasons for the recommendation and the conditions that the provincial director would recommend be set under section 105 to the young person, a parent of the young person and the Attorney General and give a copy of the notice to the youth justice court.

Application to court for review of recommendation

(3) If notice of a recommendation is made under subsection (2) with respect to a youth sentence imposed on a young person, the youth justice court shall, if an application for review is made by the young person, the young person's parent or the Attorney General within ten days after service of the notice, review the youth sentence without delay.

Subsections 94(7), (9) to (12) and (14) to (19) apply

(4) Subject to subsection (5), subsections 94(7) (no review of appeal pending), (9) to (12) (progress reports) and (14) to (19) (provisions respecting notice and decision of the youth justice court) apply, with any modifications that the circumstances require, in respect of reviews made under this section and any notice required under subsection 94(14) shall also be given to the provincial director.

If no application for review made under subsection (3)

(5) A youth justice court that receives a notice under subsection (2) shall, if no application for a review is made under subsection (3),

(*a*) order the release of the young person and place the young person under conditional supervision in accordance with section 105, having regard to the recommendations of the provincial director; or

(*b*) if the court considers it advisable, order that the young person not be released.

For greater certainty, an order under this subsection may be made without a hearing.

Notice when no release ordered

(6) When a youth justice court orders that the young person not be released under paragraph (5)(*b*), it shall cause a notice of its order to be given to the provincial director without delay.

Provincial director may request review	(7) When the provincial director is given a notice under subsection (6), he or she may request a review under this section.
When provincial director requests a review	(8) When the provincial director requests a review under subsection (7),(*a*) the provincial director shall cause any notice that may be directed by rules of court applicable to the youth justice court or, in the absence of such a direction, at least five clear days notice of the review to be given in writing to the young person, a parent of the young person and the Attorney General; and
	(*b*) the youth justice court shall review the youth sentence without delay after the notice required under paragraph (*a*) is given.
Conditional supervision	**105. *(1) The provincial director of the province in which a young person on whom a youth sentence under paragraph 42(2)(o), (q) or (r) has been imposed is held in custody or, if applicable, with respect to whom an order has been made under subsection 104(1) (continuation of custody), shall cause the young person to be brought before the youth justice court at least one month before the expiry of the custodial portion of the youth sentence. The court shall, after giving the young person an opportunity to be heard, by order, set the conditions of the young person's conditional supervision.***

Conditions to be
included in order

(2) The youth justice court shall include in the order under subsection (1) the following conditions, namely, that the young person

(*a*) keep the peace and be of good behaviour;

(*b*) appear before the youth justice court when required by the court to do so;

(*c*) report to the provincial director immediately on release, and then be under the supervision of the provincial director or a person designated by the youth justice court;

(*d*) inform the provincial director immediately on being arrested or questioned by the police;

(*e*) report to the police, or any named individual, as instructed by the provincial director;

(*f*) advise the provincial director of the young person's address of residence on release and after release report immediately to the clerk of the youth justice court or the provincial director any change

(i) in that address,

(ii) in the young person's normal occupation, including employment, vocational or educational training and volunteer work,

(iii) in the young person's family or financial situation, and

(iv) that may reasonably be expected to affect the young person's ability to comply with the conditions of the order;

(*g*) not own, possess or have the control of any weapon, ammunition, prohibited ammunition, prohibited device or explosive substance, except as authorized by the order; and

(*h*) comply with any reasonable instructions that the provincial director considers necessary in respect of any condition of the conditional supervision in order to prevent a breach of that condition or to protect society.

Other conditions (3) In setting conditions for the purposes of subsection (1), the youth justice court may include in the order the following conditions, namely, that the young person

(*a*) on release, travel directly to the young person's place of residence, or to any other place that is noted in the order;

(*b*) make reasonable efforts to obtain and maintain suitable employment;

(*c*) attend school or any other place of learning, training or recreation that is appropriate, if the court is satisfied that a suitable program is available for the young person at such a place;

(*d*) reside with a parent, or any other adult that the court considers appropriate, who is willing to provide for the care and maintenance of the young person;

(*e*) reside in any place that the provincial director may specify;

(*f*) remain within the territorial jurisdiction of one or more courts named in the order;

(*g*) **comply with conditions set out in the order that support and address the needs of the young person and promote the reintegration of the young person into the community**; and

(*h*) comply with any other conditions set out in the order that the court considers appropriate, including conditions for securing the young person's good conduct and for preventing the young person from repeating the offence or committing other offences.

Temporary conditions (4) When a provincial director is required under subsection (1) to cause a young person to be brought before the youth justice court but cannot do so for reasons beyond the young person's control, the provincial director shall so advise the youth justice court and the court shall, by order, set any temporary conditions for the young person's conditional supervision that are appropriate in the circumstances.

Conditions to be set at first opportunity (5) When an order is made under subsection (4), the provincial director shall bring the young person before the youth justice court as soon after the order is made as the circumstances permit and the court shall then set the conditions of the young person's conditional supervision.

Report (6) For the purpose of setting conditions under this section, the youth justice court shall require the provincial director to cause to be prepared, and to submit to the youth justice court, a report setting out any information that may be of assistance to the court.

Provisions apply (7) Subsections 99(2) to (7) (provisions respecting reports and notice) and 104(4) (ordering appearance of young person) apply, with any modifications that the circumstances require, in respect of any proceedings held under subsection (1).

Provisions apply (8) Subsections 56(1) to (4) (provisions respecting probation orders), (7) (notice to appear) and (8) (warrant in default) and section 101 (review of youth justice court decision) apply, with any modifications that the circumstances require, in respect of an order made under subsection (1).

Implications
While custody may be part of the disposition set upon a young person, it is still the ultimate focus of a healthy return to society where both public interests and individual interests are attended to in ways that support healthy community.

Programs

Community-based programs

157. The Attorney General of Canada or a minister designated by the lieutenant governor in council of a province may establish the following types of community-based programs:

(a) programs that are an alternative to judicial proceedings, such as victim-offender reconciliation programs, mediation programs and restitution programs;

(b) programs that are an alternative to detention before sentencing, such as bail supervision programs; and

(c) programs that are an alternative to custody, such as intensive support and supervision programs, and programs to carry out attendance orders.

Implications

The focus here is of course community building. The opportunity that is being presented within this component of the legislation is to gather people together; professionals, community members, people who have known conflict with the law, people in conflict with the law, and listen to one another an dcreate with one another ways that will support community integration,k community well-being. The quesitons we need to ask include:
- What do we truly mean when we say integration?
- What do we truly mean when we say community?
- How will we know when true transformation is taking place?
- Who will take the initiative to set the stage for transformative opportunities?
- When will the opportunities for community-building commence?
- Have community-builidng, restorative justice philosphy and practices already started?
  If so, where are they? How do we link up with them?
- What questions are missing?
- Who is not being represented here at this meeitng?

A great many people think they are thinking {changing},
when they are memely rearranging their prejudices.
William James 1842-1910

#49
"Honouring Gifts"

With eagle feather in hand he raises it and with a quite voice he says thank you to those 7 gifts—love, respect, truth, honest, humility, bravery, wisdom, for guiding him in life.

Victim Offender Reconciliation Program

Russell Kelly

In The Beginning

Present Day

Hello and good day! My name is Russell Kelly, it is May 2004, I have now been happily married for over 12 years and presently I am looking for work in the areas of security, surveillance, investigation, and the judicial field. Last spring I graduated from the Law and Security Administration program at Conestoga College in Kitchener, Ontario. In my spare time I volunteer for Community Justice Initiatives of Waterloo Region. My volunteering involves Community Mediation, Victim Offender Reconciliation, guest speaking engagements concerning Restorative Justice, and generally promoting Community Justice Initiatives and its' many programs. This promotion is done through radio, television and newspaper interviews.

This year celebrates 30 years of Restorative Justice in Canada. A book on the history of Community Justice Initiatives of Waterloo Region is to be released this spring. The author of this book interviewed many people including myself in order to give a clear picture of the history of Restorative Justice and how it all started in Kitchener, Ontario. You may be wondering why I was interviewed for the book and this is something I am willing to share with you.

My formative years

My seven siblings and I were raised in Mount Forest, Ontario. When I was six years old, my father died, leaving my mother to look after her eight children. At the young age of fifteen my mother also died and my eldest brother became my official guardian. At the time, he had just gotten married and was putting his life back on track because he had made a few bad choices and poor decisions. Dad was not there to guide him and keep him out of trouble. This was a scary time for me and a challenging time for him. While I lived under his roof I lived under his law because he did not want me to make the same mistakes and I respect him for that. He did his best!

Feeling unjustly victimized, and deeply hurt at the loss of my mother I was a confused teenager. In 1971, there weren't programs in place to properly deal with grief and the trauma that I felt when I lost my mother. At the age of fifteen, I still hadn't understood (or should I say - accepted) the loss of my father. Sure, I went to the school guidance counselor, only to have appointments set up to see a psychiatrist who in turn only told me that I was not crazy. He did not help me deal with my emotions and anger. Talking to my siblings about my problems was not an option and our aunts and uncles didn't have what you would call close ties with our family. Looking for ways to deal with my emotional pain I turned to drugs and alcohol.

Bad Habit Turns To Vice

By 1974, I had developed a strong reliance on drugs and alcohol as well as the people that could feed my established habit. Since the grief and pain wasn't dealt with in a positive way and vented properly, I would get very hostile when I got drunk and often it felt as though my head was going to explode. It was difficult to think clearly and rationalize sensibly. There were times that I would end up in fights and very often have vague memories of what happened the night before. Black-outs were a common occurrence. I was not the person that I wanted to be, nor the person that my parents wanted me to be. They sure wouldn't have been proud of me. I was on a path to nowhere and life went on.

One night in May of 1974, I went to Elmira, Ontario, to visit some of my so-called friends. Of course that visit was to drink and get drunk. My friend and I went for a drive with a case or two of beer. We drove around the back roads for hours drinking beer and getting drunker by the minute. It was after mid-night when we got pulled over by the police. Things were different back then, the officer took what was left of our beer, gave us a stern warning and told us to go home.

A Crazy Senseless Night

We made our way back into town and went to my friends apartment building. Upon arriving at the apartment building, my friend suggested we go raise some hell. Not being of sound mind, I shrugged my shoulders and said something like, "What the hell, why not?" I asked my friend what he had in mind and he suggested that we proceed to wreak havoc and destroy whatever was in our path. I am not proud of what we did that night in Elmira, but I'll tell you anyway. I had a switchblade and my accomplice had a sharp kitchen knife that we used to slash 24 car tires. We slashed car seats and destroyed a car radiator. Rocks were thrown through large plate glass windows in homes and the front window at the local beer store. A boat was pulled into the street, punctured and overturned. A gazebo was damaged, a flashing light at an intersection was damaged and a cross was broken from a display case at a local church. Side windows and car windshields were smashed with beer bottles. A garden table was thrown into a fishpond and a fence destroyed. In all, 22 properties received damage. All this happened in about a two hour span from about 3:00 a.m. to 5:00 a.m. When we had enough of this craziness we headed back to the apartment and passed-out.

Busted

The police were pounding at the door at about 7:00 a.m. Someone had seen us running through the back-yards and gave a description to the police. It didn't take long to figure out the two young men that were pulled over the previous night were the likely suspects. My accomplice and I were detained in separate rooms for questioning. The police did not use the good cop - bad cop routine with us. They just asked us if we were the ones that committed all the damage the previous night. I knew we messed up big time and I felt terrible about it, so I admitted my part in the crime spree. However, my accomplice was not as forthcoming with his guilt. Indeed, he did confess to his part of the crime after learning of my confession. We both knew that we messed up severely and it was only right to own up to our mistakes and face the consequences.

Judicial System Takes A Turn

At the time of "The Elmira Case", Mark Yantzi was a probation officer and a volunteer with the Mennonite Central Committee in Kitchener. Mark was handed our case and in a meeting with other volunteer members he suggested, "Wouldn't it be neat for these offenders to meet with their victims?" The offenders could be accountable for their actions and repair the harm done. Mark felt there could be some therapeutic value in this approach. Yet, having this novel idea, he didn't think the idea was any more than just that. Another volunteer, Dave Worth, told Mark that his idea was a great one and it should not only be further investigated, but to suggest it to the judge. Mark attached an addendum to the back of the pre-sentence report for the judge. Judge Gordon McConnell saw no precedence in law to allow this idea. However, Judge McConnell was tired of the revolving door of justice and was looking for a new approach for justice. There was no basis in law to order my accomplice and I to do this, so Mark asked us and advised it would be best for all concerned. My accomplice and I decided it was the right thing to do. If we did not go along with this novel suggestion - we were sure to see the inside of jail for a long time. Having agreed to meet our victims opened the door for the judge to include this as part of our probation order.

Meeting Our Victims

Meeting our victims was one of the hardest things I had ever done in my entire life. Accompanied by Mark Yantzi (our probation officer) and Dave Worth (a volunteer), we walked up to the victims front door to apologize, hear what the victims had to say, determine the amount of restitution, ask for forgiveness and assure the victims that they were not targeted. It was a random act of vandalism.

Some victims offered forgiveness while others wanted to give us a good whipping. Nonetheless, we survived meeting the victims of our crime spree and returned a couple of months later with certified cheques to restore the amount of out-of-pocket expenses not covered by insurance. The total damage was around $2,200; my accomplice and myself each had to pay $550 restitution and each paid a $200 fine. As well, we were placed on 18 months probation. I thought that was the end of that shameful part of my life. Little did I know what would become of this judicial experiment. Unknowingly to me the Victim Offender Reconciliation Program was born.

Finding Out

Due to a back injury caused by many years of factory work involving heavy repetitive lifting, I was forced to change my type of work. My choice of new employment would be the security field. I was enrolled in the Law and Security Administration program at Conestoga College in Kitchener, Ontario.

We often had guest speakers give us presentations on various topics. One day while sitting in a Community Services class we had a guest speaker from Community Justice Initiatives of Waterloo Region in Kitchener. Julie Friesen started the story by saying that a probation officer by the name of Mark Yantzi was handed an unusual case in 1974. I thought to myself, Mark Yantzi was my probation officer in 1974. Then Julie went on to talk about two drunken teenagers that went on a vandalism spree in the town of Elmira. That is when it hit me. I mean it really hit me! I knew she was talking about me and I was overwhelmed, big-time! My palms were sweating and my heart was pounding so much that I was having trouble taking notes. My face felt like it was quite red - I guess from all the blood rushing through my body. Time seemed to pass very slowly. Julie mentioned that her office tried to contact the two offenders for the 25th anniversary, but they could not be located. I thought to myself, wait a minute; I only live twenty minutes away. It was a two hour class and after much deliberation, I decided to tell Julie who I am. We exchanged numbers and the next thing I knew, I was talking to Mark in his office after 28 years.

A Time To Give Back

All this had made such an impression on me that I joined Community Justice Initiatives, took the mediation training and have spent over 250 volunteer hours in criminal court advising Crown Attorneys', defence lawyers, victims and offenders of the cases appropriate for VORP. In addition, my spare time allows me to do other mediation cases and promote Restorative Justice philosophy, the agency for which I volunteer and its' many programs. As well, I enjoy sharing my story with all that will listen.

Like I said earlier in this article, "I am not proud of what I did; however, I am extremely proud of what has become of it". It still amazes me that something so wrong could result in something so good that has affected many, many lives in a positive way.

In closing, I would like to thank the countless number of people that contributed to enhancing and fine tuning the program to where it is today. This includes but not limited to the many volunteers, teachers, judges, and others in the judicial system; as well as the many victims and offenders that have chosen to participate in mediation to resolve conflict. It is the better way to go!

By the way, I applied for and received my pardon from the Government of Canada prior to starting my college program. This allowed me a clear police records check which in turn allowed me to volunteer. Isn't it funny how some things work out?

Community Justice Initiatives: 1974 - Present

Community Justice Initiatives (CJI) is a non-profit organization, known world-wide as having started the first restorative justice program. We provide services in conflict resolution, sexual trauma and support for women after they leave prison. We serve everyone, including families, friends, groups, neighbours, schools, and the workplace. All of our programs are founded on principles of restorative justice, a way of addressing conflict and crime that engages the person who caused the harm and people who were affected by the harm.Our programs are made possible through volunteers, donations and individual and public support. Services are available free or for a nominal fee.

Community Justice Initiatives (CJI) of Waterloo Region, Kitchener, Ontario, has grown extensively since its' humble beginnings in 1974. Presently there are many programs that have developed over the years that help the community and society as a whole to heal from the harms of conflict and crime.

They are as follows:

- **RESOLVE** provides mediation and conflict resolution services for individuals and groups in our community and for the justice system.
- **REVIVE** provides group support for women, men, and children who are recovering from sexual trauma. Revive also supports people who have offended sexually in making safe, healthy choices.
- **STRIDE** assists women in making the transition from prison to their community by engaging and involving the community.

As well, Community Justice Initiatives has a program that addresses **Elder Abuse**.

For more information on Community Justice Initiatives you can access the web site at: www.cjiwr.com or email info@cjiwr.com

For additional information or questions about the article or my involvement in Restorative Justice please contact Russ Kelly by email at: rdkelly@sympatico.ca

Finally, the Victim/Offender Mediation program has spread to over 80 countries of the European Union as well as the United States, New Zealand, Australia, Africa, South America and others.

Frequently Asked Questions

Q: *Is this not just a soft way of dealing with the offender?*

A: No. Quite the opposite! A common refrain from people who have gone through the circle process (as offender) is that this was the toughest thing they have ever had to do. The circle was also the most meaningful thing that they could have done. Many offenders find the court system less stessful. The tough part of the circle for the offender comes on a number of levels:
   a) the individual must sit face to face with the person who has been victimized by the behavior of the offender;
   b) the individual must listen to the exact words and feelings of the person victimized by their behavior;
   c) the individual must hear the accounts of other people affected by the event, including the effect the behavior has had on their own family members;
   d) the individual must articulate to everyone in the circle how they became involved in the event, what they were thinking when they engaged in the event, what it has been like for them since the event, who they have seen affected by the event and ultimately what do they see themselves as being capable of doing to repair the harm they have caused.

Having heard from everyone in the circle it is quite common for the person in the offending role to state: "I never realized that I affected so many people." As one person who went through the circle in the role of the offender stated "what came out of this was the truth about why I did what I did, I certainly wasn't expecting that to happen." This process is very much in contrast to the criminal court process, where the offender does not necessarily speak for him/herself... rather the lawyer does the speaking. The victim has no real voice in the process, as the crown represents them, and in some instances the victim may not even know the court proceeding has been undertaken.

Q: *Won't the circle process revictimize the person who was already victimized?*

A: No. A key aspect of the circle is giving voice to the person victimized. A common misconception is that victims do not want to have anything to do with the event or the people connected to it. In reality, the victim often is wanting the following:
   a) they wished that the event had never happened, but given that it has…they want

to know why they were the victims of this act;
b) they want an authentic apology from the person who did the act... they want to know that the person is sincerely sorry for what has transpired... and to know that the offending behavior will come to a stop.

Within the circle process, statements common to people who had been in the role of victim include:

• "I really felt that people heard me";
• "I really felt that I had power to create a solution on how to deal with this issue";
• "I realized that I am not alone in this, that there are people here to support me".

Q: Won't the offender take the circle process as an opportunity to pretend they are contrite and remorseful? This way they won't have to go on to a more 'serious' manner of being dealt with.

A: Anyone has the capacity to pretend one thing while holding quite another feeling. Often in the criminal court process, the offender is coached on being contrite by the persons representing him. Within the circle, however, the focus is on the offender's capacity to repair the harm. The focus is not the flaws and blameworthiness of the offender. This sets a context in place that all human beings need opportunity to be accepted by others. Through this process the person must demonstrate that they do, in fact, have capacities and attributes that are praiseworthy. The offender then does not need to hide behind a 'wall' of defense postures, because no one is "out to get him"... rather people are out to see his strengths. Lastly, there is the emotional aspect of a circle. Repeatedly, people who have gone through the circle process have commented on the sincere emotion that surfaces.

Q: Is this very time consuming in contrast to the criminal court process?

A: No. Where circles may be convened in 3 to 5 weeks from the time of the event, the same event may take 6 months to over a year to be cleared through the criminal court process. A Circle may take only an hour or two to complete, while a court case, with its barrage of witnesses, and possible need for jury selection, may run on for a day or more. In instances of a guilty plea, the entire court process may last less than 15 minutes.

Q: What happens in the instance where criminal charges have been laid? Are you not to proceed because you might "contaminate the evidence"?

A: Where you have an agreement with the police and court/crowns office and there is the following:

> Undertaking and Waiver of Delays, you may proceed with the circle and the outcomes of the circle are forwarded to the crown attorney's office.

The circle process is not in lieu of the court process. The circle process is not in lieu of the suspension process. In instances where a circle was facilitated and the outcomes were mutually arrived at and agreed to, and this was forwarded to the crown attorney, this does not result in automatic dismissal of the charges before the court. The goal of the circle is how to mutually arrive at steps that can help repair the harm that has been done. It is not a "carrot to be held out", for this would only diminish the authenticity of the circle process.

Q: Should circles only be limited to events such as theft under, in effect property crimes and not any behavior beyond this?

A: No. Circles can be implemented in a number of instances. Circles have been facilitated for assault, theft, threats, sexual assault, break and enter, vandalism... in essence, in any instances where harm has been exacted and people want to pursue a process to help repair the harm.

According to Anne Schneider who facilitated a circle dealing with domestic violence she had this to offer: "As I was doing the circle I, at least in the early stages, worried that the focus was not staying with the abuse and in fact I even wondered if I hadn't done my pre work well enough because they weren't talking about "what they were supposed to talk about." Fortunately, I was able to let go and accepted that they were talking about what they needed to talk about. I also had some worries that the questions were awkward and weren't getting at the right issues. Again as the process continued I began to think and feel that the questions didn't really matter - that they were just a container to provide some structure and safety and that what needed to be said would get said.

As most people involved know, I was worried about how a fair and do-able plan would evolve without a fair bit of negotiation and mediation. It did. The building blocks and the language for the plan started coming out almost immediately as I watched various players listening and thinking intently.

I really liked the feeling in the circle. There wasn't a shirking of responsibility, but it wasn't burdening (the person who committed the offending behavior) with blame and thereby immobilizing him. Rather the "this is what you did" message was really balance out by his strengths which seemed to give him the tools and allow him to draw on the positive energy that he needed to take the next steps. I think others felt this positive energy in the circle as well. The final comments were all very positive and the feeling of apprehension and anxiety that was present when people first came into the room was certainly gone."

I think that the format with everyone responding to the same questions brings a real equality to the process, all people and their ideas are valued and none are more important than others are. Some leveling took place."

Q: Are not peer mediation, conflict resolution, restorative justice circles all just the same thing but with different names?

A: No. These endeavors share similar outcomes: a healthy safe community, but there are differences within the process. Bringing two youths into the office to discuss a fight that occurred in the school yard and coming up with ways to ensure that it will not happen again has a shared outcome with the restorative justice process, but the path is different. Restorative justice, when employed, draws upon not only the principles involved (the offender and the victim), but it will also draw upon supporters that may range from staff to family members to extended family, to community members.

Q: Do you need to see remorse from the person who did the offending behavior, before considering convening a circle?

A: While it is certainly the preferred state (a person who is remorseful for their behavior) it may not preclude their involvement if they do not initially show remorse, if these elements exist:

a) the person agrees they did the offending behavior;

b) the person who has been victimized by the behavior is aware of this but still would like the opportunity to pursue steps to repair harm;

c) the supporters of the person who did the offending behavior are in agreement to the circle and want to take steps to help repair the harm that has been done;

d) there is agreement that people need to be held accountable for their behaviors and part of that accountability is to see and hear from those who have been directly affected by their behavior;

e) it is crucial to remain clear about one of the principles of the circle... the pursuit of creating steps to repair the harm, not about the pursuit of blameworthiness. Consequently, there is more latitude for creatively exploring how one can repair the harm.

f) there are also instances where the offender may in fact also be a victim and this may contribute to the person's seeming unwillingness to show remorse about the event. It is incumbent upon the facilitator to gather as much information as possible about what did transpire

Q: What happens if the person who did the offending behavior does not follow through on the agreed to outcomes?

A: Surprisingly the outcomes tend to be quite straightforward and doable, and most often include an authentic apology, which tends to take place right within the circle. Beyond the apology, it is common for people to feel their needs have been met simply by being in the circle and hearing everyone's story. However, in the event of an outcome not being achieved, the monitors would need to meet in order to discuss how it could be achieved. It is important to frame the outcome that is being addressed in the form of: "how to…"

Within the Family

Together in life they pray. It is within the Sweatlodge that they call upon the spirits of each doorway, and as those spirits near the energy around them stirs. As the Grandfathers (hot rocks) sit in the pit in front of them they share their breath/words of life with them. They are the Seven Grandfathers also known as the seven prophecies of life. To the East they ask that Great Eagle to carry their thoughts and prayers up to the Creator. They ask that those who have passed on and who have carved this path of life to be remembered, as well to look out for those to come, our future generations. It is that balance they search for, for they know to pray first for those least fortunate, sick and weak. Together they heal and it is within this womb their hearts come together as one. It is the power that surrounds them, that protects them, guides them but yet teaches us of how strong the elements of life can be.

Concluding Musings

A group of us have been involved in facilitating training of restorative justice since 1994. Some of us formed a 'team' to write this book: Restorative Justice –Transforming Society. As we reflect on a decade of work, we had a conversation - musings about where we see Restorative Justice as we publish our book in 2005.

Lynn Zammit: A decade ago, we were swimming up stream. That is no longer true. When we talk to people today, there is new a willingness to explore this new way of doing justice. There is more openness to explore community-building. People are open now; I am not sure why. Perhaps it is dissatisfaction with the way things have been done when it comes to dealing with at-risk-youth.

Rick Owens: What I have seen is a growing mindfulness of relationships, needs and capacities. A decade ago, those were 'eccentric' ideas. Now, we speak more in terms of what actually can and should be done to resolve conflicts and differences. And we talk about our capacity to do that, regardless of the labels that have been affixed to some of us.

Now, when situations arise, 'circles' are becoming closer to a first response, rather than an afterthought. That is a huge shift. I have learned to appreciate that cultural change requires time and patience.

Randy Charboneau: I've been through the whole other process of retributive ways and institutions. I've seen first hand what prisons do to people - to the human spirit. I saw and experienced a system where neither the victim nor the offender ever had a voice. The only people who seemed to have voices were the police, the judges, and crown attorneys. As a result, be you offender or victim, you were just shut down. The offender and victim both become numbers and that's all. When you walk into that place (prison) you don't even have a name or an identity: you are just that number. That is real depth and impact of the retributive system.

Lynn: We've all worked or lived in big systems, but now I see that people are trying to make connections. And making connections is the opposite of the big retributive system.

Randy: I agree, but I also feel that people are still frightened, or at least leery of trying new things, especially when we are talking about crime, or youth into trouble. Still, I am hopeful.

Art Lockhart: Shedding favourite ways of thinking and doing can be pretty challenging. There is the wonderful saying by the Chinese philosopher, Lao Tzu: "Treat big things in small ways." Our discussion about connections makes me think that just maybe the 'big system stuff' is no longer seen as the best, or only at least not the only way to treat complex issues such as youth in conflict and crime. Just maybe there is a new willingness to explore the power and potential of 'small ways' – of people ways.

Rick: For us (Griffin Centre), restorative justice is about transforming how **we** are in relation to the children and families with whom we work. It is about how we see ourselves, them, and the communities in which we all live. Restorative justice says the world is too complex to reduce to simple categories, labels and diagnoses. At some times, each of us are aggressors, "offenders", the ones who cause harm. At other times, sometimes even in the same situation, we are the "victims", the ones who are harmed. Our goal is to see and respond to people/situations in ways that invite reflection and change, recognizing that we too are sometimes the 'problem'. We strive to make community in and through every relationship - every encounter.

Art: Thinking further about change and transformation, in our last facilitators meeting, people asked about the history of oppression. They asked how (if at all) this is played out within the circle process. For example: are there issues of oppression that need attention when the facilitator is white and all the participants are black; or the facilitator is black and all the participants are white? Or, what is the experience when the facilitator is a white Anglo-male and the participants are Muslim; or when the facilitator is female and the principles in the circle are male. How are these experiences attended to?

Rick: We must be careful about respecting the extraordinary diversity of cultures and practices. Meaning well isn't good enough. With any system of values, beliefs and practices, good intentions can cause harm if we are not careful. We must be critical and vigilant for the ways in which we inevitably 'trespass' against each other. This can happen even when we are doing something as important as building community.

Art: For me, the circle has always been about uniting and then transcending the implied barriers and boundaries. In a circle, we are all together. In many ways, the facilitator becomes invisible; the participants have the open space to create magic together.

Lynn: The facilitator has a silent voice. The facilitator does not bring their own story to the circle. Their voice and role is to unveil everyone else's voice - their stories. For that reason, I don't see why the facilitator's race or colour matters.

Art: The key for me is that good facilitators will have created relationships with all the participants in advance of the circle. While establishing those relationships, the role of the facilitator must be clarified: to create the opportunity, the open space, where everyone's voice will be heard.   When facilitators are the 'silent voice', and create a safe space for everyone's voice, then, and only then, is there an opportunity to help repair the harm that has taken place.

Randy: My thought is that, when a person states that I need to have someone of my own race facilitate my circle, that person is the source of their own oppression. The day you say I cannot have a person of another race facilitate/mediate a process about healing, is the day you are oppressing yourself. The ultimate goal is to make relationships, acknowledge relationships. Our community has different races, different cultures, different religions. No one group has ownership over another; no one knows more about goodness than another. The elders in their teachings, say that the day that we put ownership on anything, for example when we say we own that circle process; we own the sweat lodge; we own mother earth; that is the day we lose that ownership.

Lynn: You are reminding me of a quote that illustrates the similarities, which really exist in the religions, cultures, we might consider different and for me this is strength of the circle process, it is saying that through understanding our uniqueness we can also find and build on our similarities. The quote I have over my desk reads:

The Golden Rule

BAHA'I FAITH
Lay not on any soul a load that you would not wish to be laid upon you, and desire not for anyone the things you would not desire for yourself. -Baha'u'llah, Gleanings

HINDUISM
This is the sum of duty: do not do to others what would cause pain if done to you.
– Mahabharata 5:1517

BUDDHISM
Treat not others in ways that you yourself would find hurtful. –Udana-Varga 5.18

CONFUCIANISM
One word which sums up the basis of all good conduct…loving kindness. Do not do to others what you do not want done to yourself. –Confucius Analects 15.23

TAOISM
Regard your neighbour's gain as your own gain, and your neighbour's loss as your own loss. – T'ai Shang Kan Ying P'ien, 213-218

SIKHISM
I am a stranger to no one; and no one is a stranger to me. Indeed, I am a friend to all.
-Guru Granth Sahib, pg. 1299

CHRISTIANITY
In everything, do to others as you would have them do to you; for this is the law and the prophets. –Jesus, Matthew 7:12

UNITARIANISM
We affirm and promote respect for the interdependent web of all existence of which we are a part. –Unitarian principle

NATIVE SPIRITUALITY
We are as much alive as we keep the earth alive. –Chief Dan George

ZOROASTRIANISM
Do not do unto others whatever is injurious to yourself. –Shayast-na-Shayast 13.29

JAINISM
One should treat all creatures in the world as one would like to be treated. –Mahavira, Sutrakritanga

JUDAISM
What is hateful to you, do not do to your neighbour. This is the whole Torah; all the rest is commentary. –Hillel, Talmud, Shabbat 31a

ISLAM
Not one of you truly believes until you wish for others what you wish for yourself. –The Prophet Muhammad, Hadith

Art: I feel that it is critical it is to encourage the circle process not to become just another program-of-the-day. It must not become a political process solely held in the mandate of political organizations. Rather, it should be understood as a process of relationship building, and community building. And as we have mentioned, there is a sacredness that surfaces in the circle experience and that must be protected.

Lynn: And the sacredness always surfaces. You cannot describe it, it just happens.

Randy: I remember when we were helping facilitate a circle with about 30 people who were dealing with school violence and bullying. Late in the meeting, a young boy spoke to the person he had harmed, "I have been wanting to tell you something for a long time, and that is 'peace man'." He just looked across the room and made the symbol for love. You are both right. Sacredness does happen in the circle.

Art: My hope is that people don't gloss over the centrality of the concepts community, of sacredness, of slowing it down. Our mission is to assist people to explore how this philosophy can be integrated into our work, into conflict intervention, and into our day-to- day life.

Lynn: At our training sessions with educators, on the last day, we ask people how they might use restorative justice in their school. We try to take the conversation away from specific facilitation skills and ask where they would use the philosophy of the process, the philosophy of relationships and community-building.   These conversations have proven to be amazing. Invariably, they generate huge lists of doable actions that would make a difference in the lives - not only of the school children, but their own lives as well.

Randy: When I am in a circle, what I always see are children who have built up layers, sometimes masks. Even though the person is an adult, I still see the child within that adult sitting in the circle. That circle is an opportunity to peel away the layers and the masks. When that happens, true and powerful connections are made. Restorative justice allows those voices to come out.

Lynn: Sometimes we do a closing activity with the students in the Choices for Youth Program. We start with a ball of yarn. The first person holding the yarn say's something positive to another person and passes the yarn to them. The yarn goes back and forth between all the youth. It looks like a spider weaving a web. Recently, I was watching a large circle of about 27 people. I was thinking about what we are really doing when we first ask the person who did the offending behaviour to start talking. At one level, we are simply passing the ball of yarn back and forth between one another. But in the process, we are not only sharing our stories, we are also creating new ones as everyone weaves the web together. It is almost as if we are watching the evolution of the Dream Catcher.

Randy: When Lynn said Dream Catcher, I had another image as well, a blanket. And this blanket provides protection. The protection is very powerful because the blanket was woven together by everyone.

Lynn: After all is said and done, having woven all these different fabrics together, the stories, the examples, the implications of the YCJA, the philosophy, it truly is simple. Gathering people together to share is profoundly simple – and simply profound.

Rick: I think that one of our key challenges will be to maintain the cultural and transformative view in the face of pressure to use simply use restorative justice as a mechanism for responding to youth crime.

Randy: The circle, for me, will always be about the sacredness of relationships.

Art: William Blake was right. To see a world in a grain of sand is to be able to step beyond boundaries that impair, and explore the connections that unite. It is our hope that with those of you who read this book will get together to explore the connections, and share your piece of dream-string, as we all keep weaving together the wonderful aesthetic imperatives. The circle is profoundly simple, and simply profound.

As the restorative justice movement evolves, we would love to hear your stories, and help create the web of stories that weave the dream catcher together. To that end, we invite you email us, and with your permission, we will celebrate the work you are doing. inclusionpress@inclusion.com

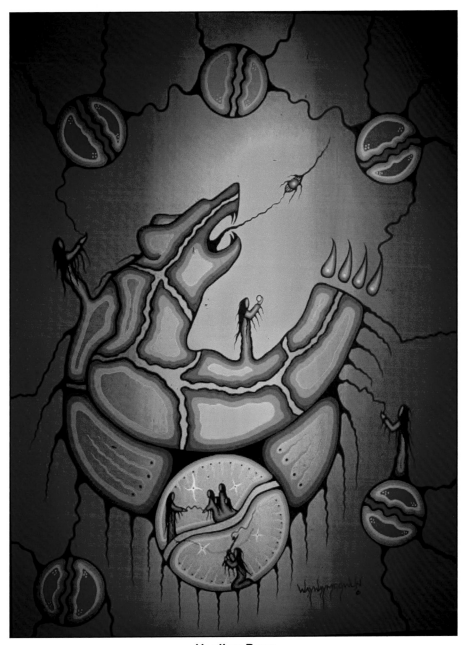

Healing Bear

As the Bear sits in the Northern Direction/Doorway he brings the element of Healing to the people through this doorway. As we pray we ask the Creator to heal all Nations of Man and this is when the Creator calls upon his helper of the North the Bear to do his most sacred work. It was the Bear that was given the knowledge of the Medicines for he is the one that digs his claws into Mother Earth with each step he takes. There are two sides to life the physical and the spiritual. And within that medicine wheel it is this man that shows us the gifts we have within. For he does the work of the creator by sharing his knowledge by voice and as well this man brings forth his spiritual knowledge. It is balance in which he delivers. So as the spirits dance high and low the healing of the Bear nurtures our souls.

Glossary

Aboriginal Justice: an approach that views a wrongdoing as a misbehaviour which requires teachings or an illness which requires healing; the purpose of a justice system in an Aboriginal society is to restore the peace and equilibrium within the community, and to reconcile the accused with his or her own conscience and with the individual or family who has been wronged.

Absolute Discharge: sec. 42(2) (b) of the YCJA; the court may order an absolute discharge of the young person if it is in the best interests of the youth and not contrary to the public interest

Acquittal: the trial of an accused results in the person being found not guilty

After Care: process to enable the youth to make a transition back into the community following a term of incarceration; this is not a universal process

Attendance Order: sec 42(2) (m) of the YCJA, where the court orders the young person to attend a non-residential program for up to 240 hours within 6 months

Bail: the security given for an accused release as a guarantee for subsequent appearance for trial. This is approved by a judicial officer and results in the release of the accused from custody, pending a trial.

"Boot Camp": correctional facility for young offenders based on a militaristic code of behaviour

"Breach of Order": refers to the circumstance(s) of the young person failing to comply with the court imposed conditions of a probation order, and can result in further charge by the probation officer, which may result in a custody disposition being imposed on the young person

Canadian Police Information Centre: known as "CPIC"; a federal police information database about offenders and their criminal records.

Case Manager: the probation officer, parole officer, social worker, youth worker, correctional officer or operational manger responsible for the co-ordination of an offender's case.

Child: a person who is under 12 years of age, administrative responsibility of Child and Family Services

Child and Family Services Act: R.S.O. 1990 Chap. C.11
The Child and Family Services Act: funding of services for children including child development, child treatment, child welfare, community support, young offenders, and child and family intervention services. It also governs the operation of children's aid societies and other agencies approved to provide these services and the licensing of residential programs.

Child And Family Service Advocacy (Advocacy Office)
Ontario's child advocate represents children and youth who are seeking or receiving services under the Child and Family Services Act, in the youth justice system, the children's mental health system, the child welfare system (children's aid societies), and provincial and demonstration schools for the deaf and blind. General Inquiry: 416-325-5669 TTY: 416-325-2648 Toll Free: 1-800-263-2841 www.pss.jus.gov.on.ca

Children's Aid Society of Toronto: Children's Aid Society of Toronto is located at 33 Charles Street East, near the Yonge / Bloor Street East intersection. This organization provides family counselling and supervision, child protection services, as well as pregnancy counselling. There are a number of branches in the Greater Toronto Area available to serve you. Please call to apply for services or for more information.   Phone: 416-924-4646

Community: the process of developing relationships which allow for the gifts and capacities of everyone to be integrated in ways that support the well-being of all community members.

Community and Family Group Conference: a coordinator invites family and friends of both the victim and the offender to participate in a discussion to explore possible ways to address the offending behaviour and outcomes for the families involved as well as the community; one of the earlier terms for restorative justice circles. George Hull Centre for Children and Families in Toronto is a leader in this area.www.georgehullcentre.on.ca

Community Service Order: sec. 42(2)(i) of the YCJA under the supervision of a probation order, the person is required to do up to a maximum of 240 hours of community service, that can be completed in twelve months

Compensation Order: see 42(2)(e) of the YCJA, where the court orders the young person to pay or make special compensation that address the unique circumstances of the offence

Concurrent Sentence: a term of imprisonment to be served simultaneously with one or more sentences

Conditional Discharge: sec. 42(2) (c) of the YCJA; the court may order a discharge of the young person on conditions. In addition, the court may require the young person to report to and be under the supervision by the provincial director

Conditional Sentence: allows an offender to serve a sentence of imprisonment in the community under court ordered conditions

Conference: Sec 19 YCJA, also may be described as Community Conference refers to the process of bringing the offender and victim together along with key people most affected by the "event" to seek a way to repair the harm that has taken place,

Correctional Officer:a person responsible for supervising offenders in a correctional facility

Correctional Services Of Canada: responsible for the administration of federal institutions (inmates serving sentences of two years or more) and federal parole offices

Criminal Record: a register of crimes maintained on persons charged with or convicted of offences under the federal Criminal Records Act

Criminogenic Society: a society that directly and indirectly supports criminal or deviant behaviour

Crown Attorney: counsel appointed by the Attorney General to prosecute persons accused of a crime

Custodial and Supervision Order: sec. 42(2)(n) of the YCJA, refers to the period of combined time of sentence to be served in a custody setting and on supervision for a maximum of 2 years (or 3 years if Criminal Code is life imprisonment) with custody being 2/3's of sentence and supervision 1/3 of sentence

Custodial and Conditional Supervision Order: sec 42(2)(o) of the YCJA concerns offences of Attempted Murder, Manslaughter, Aggravated Sexual Assault-for up to 3 years maximum with final portion of the sentence being served under supervision with conditions unless youth is "gated" see sec: 104(1)

Declaration of Principle: Sec 3 of the YCJA the guiding principles/values/beliefs which are the framework of the YCJA

Deferred Custody and Supervision: sec 42(2) (p) of the YCJA, when a young person is found guilty of an offence that is not a serious violent offence, the court may impose a sentencing option of deferred custody; while the young person serves the sentence in the community on conditions it is still considered a type of custodial sentence because breach of condition can result in the young person serving the remainder of the sentence as a custody order

Disposition: a court order that imposes a penalty when a finding of guilt has been made against the accused.

Earned Remission: the one-third reduction of an inmate's sentence due to good behavior for adult offenders in a custody facility

Electronic Monitoring: a program that monitors adult inmates serving a custodial sentence in the community by way of an electronic tracking device

Expunged: term for having one's record removed through the pardon process (see pardons)

Extrajudicial Measures: sec 4 through 10 YCJA; as with intent of alternative measures of the YOA, the aim is to deal with the young person, alleged to have committed an offence, outside the formal court process:

Extrajudicial Sanctions: sec10 of the YCJA, a court imposed action to be taken by the young person, outside formal judicial sanctions

Family Group Conference: one of the earlier terms for restorative justice circles. Key focus on family involvement in addressing the harm that has taken place. George Hull Centre for Children and Families in Toronto is a leader in this area. www.georgehullcentre.on.ca

Fine: sec. 42(2) (d) of the YCJA; impose on the young person a fine not exceeding $1,000.00 to be paid in accordance with terms laid down by the court

First Degree Murder: sec. 42(2)(q) of the YCJA; impose on the young person 10 years maximum custody followed by conditional supervision; Second Degree Murder impose 7 years maximum with 4 years maximum custody followed by conditional supervision

Freedom of Information Act: legislation designed to provide individuals access to information contained in the records of government ministries, agencies, banks, commissions and corporations

Juvenile Delinquency Act: dealt with youth age 7 to 16 and, was in force from 1908 until it was replaced by the Young Offenders Act in 1983

Intensive Support and Supervision: sec 42(2)(l) of the YCJA, requires the agreement of the Provincial Director and program approved by the Provincial Director, focuses on the treatment of serious violent offenders with special attention to sections 42(7)(a); 42(7)(b); 42(7)(c) and 42(7)(d)

Intermittent Sentence: a court imposed sentence not to exceed ninety days, to be served intermittently (weekends)

Level of Service Inventory-Ontario Revision: a standardized and objective assessment based on criminogenic and social history factors (i.e. criminal record, education etc.) it identifies the offender's risk to re-offend and is used to determine program delivery needs of the offender

Living Unit/Unit/Range/Pod: inmate accommodation areas in correctional institutions

Maori Justice: Aboriginal justice of New Zealand, aligned with Aboriginal justice in Canada, one of the principal initiating philosophies of the contemporary restorative justice movement. The term for Maori custom of New Zealand is tikanga as a derivative of 'tika' - that which is fair, true, just or 'rightness' Generally speaking, the Maori value system is described in terms of criteria like whanaungatanga, manaakitanga, aroha, rangatiratanga or utu, the maintenance of harmony and balance.

Ministry of the Attorney General: responsible for providing a fair and accessible justice system which reflects the needs of the diverse communities it serves across government and the province. It strives to manage the justice system in an equitable, affordable and accessible way throughout the province.

The Ministry delivers and administers a wide range of justice services including:

1. administering approximately 115 statutes;

2. conducting criminal proceedings throughout Ontario;

3. providing legal advice to, and conducting litigation on behalf of, all government ministries and many agencies, boards and tribunals;

4. providing advice on, and drafting, all legislation and regulations; and

5. coordinating and administering court services throughout Ontario.

The Office of the Public Guardian and Trustee, the Children's Lawyer (formerly called the Official Guardian), and the Special Investigations Unit (SIU) all fall within MAG's responsibilities. The Ministry also funds Legal Aid Ontario which is administered by an independent Board. www.attorneygeneral.jus.gov. on.ca

Ministry of Children and Youth Services: as well as providing services for children (birth to age 12) the ministry provides youth justice services to youth, aged 12 to 17 at the time of their offence, who are charged with or convicted of criminal or provincial offences.

The government is committed to a youth justice system that builds safer communities by holding youth accountable for their actions, and helps young people in conflict with the law get their lives back on track to become contributing members of society. See: www.children.gov.on.ca

Ministry of Community and Social Services: responsible for a wide range of community services including: aboriginal healing, homelessness, domestic violence, developmental disabilities. www.cfcs.gov.on.ca

The Ministry of Community Safety and Correctional Services: responsible for ensuring that Ontario's communities is supported and protected by law enforcement and public safety systems that are safe, secure, effective, efficient and accountable. Responsible for addressing people age18 and over, who come into conflict with the law. See www.pss.jus.gov.on.ca

Mixed sentences: and aggregate sentence consisting of a combined young offender and adult sentence

Narrative Therapy: Michael White and David Epston were the first to envision therapy in this way and they have developed most of the ideas and practices. It's a therapy which links the personal and the political - to connect personal troubles with social issues. it looks at how a person/family's position in life (for example: race, class, culture) influences how the person or family sees itself or is seen by others and what that means for the way their lives are then lived. Information about ourselves, each other and the world is transmitted through stories told in our families and communities. At Oolagen, we are working with youth and families experiencing troubles to challenge the stories about their lives and relationships which are oppressive, to access stories of their own competence and survival abilities and to discover and build upon a new, more hopeful view of themselves. Oolagen is also interested in restorative justice because it fits with narrative ideas - it provides an opportunity for youth and families to resolve conflicts in ways that repair harm. In so doing, clients are given the opportunity to experience themselves as a person/people who can make a positive impact on their lives and others (instead of simply experiencing themselves as a "bad person" who must be punished). This can be the starting point for a new story about themselves and their lives. One of the leading agencies in Canada promoting and working with narrative therapy is Oolagen in Toronto. wwwocs@oolagen.org

Office for Victims of Crime (OVC): As part of the Victims' Justice Action Plan, on June 11, 2001, the Office for Victims of Crime (OVC) 416-326-1682. became a permanent advisory agency to advise the Attorney General on ways to ensure that the principles set out in the Victims' Bill of Rights are respected. The OVC also offers advise with respect to: the development, implementation and maintenance of provincial standards for services for victims of crime; the use of the Victims' Justice Fund to provide and improve services for victims of crime; research and education on the treatment of victims of crime and ways to prevent further victimization; matters of legislation and policy on the treatment of victims of crime and on the prevention of further victimization.

Ontario Board Of Parole: the releasing authority for adult inmates serving sentences of up to two years less one day in Ontario who are eligible for parole. When released from custody after serving one-third of his/her sentence, the inmate becomes a parolee and is supervised by a probation/parole officer

Open Custody: sec. 83, 84 and 85 of the YCJA, community residential centre where young offenders receive supervision and program/ treatment opportunities

Open Detention: see sec 83, 84 and 85 of the YCJA

Pardon: the process of having one's criminal record sealed and set apart from other criminal records, thereafter through the record will not be disclosed to any person without the specific approval of the Solicitor General of Canada.
       NOTE: contrary to popular belief a youth's record is not automatically destroyed once the youth turns 18. A youth record is expunged one year after the finding of guilt for an absolute

discharge and three years after receiving a conditional discharge; where there was a disposition other than a discharge the record will remain for 3 years from the end of the disposition, and in the case of a more serious offence the record is maintained for a period of 5 years following the completion of the sentence

Source: Clemency and Pardon Division of the National Parole Board at 1-800-874-2652 or Director Identification Services Royal Canadian Mounted Police P.O. Box 8885 Ottawa ON K1G-3M8

Parole (provincial): the conditional release of an adult inmate to the community by the Ontario Parole Board, while supervised by a probation/parole officer. Provincial parole is currently being phased out of the provincial criminal justice system.

Parolee: an adult offender who is conditionally released from custody to complete his/her sentence in the community under the supervision of a probation/parole officer

Plan of Care: a supervision plan for young offenders developed by the case management team in cooperation with the offender which recognizes the specific cultural, linguistic, treatment and behavioral needs of young persons in custody

Pre-Disposition Report: a court ordered report prepared by a probation officer to assist the judge in determining the appropriate disposition for a young offender

Pre-Sentence Report: a court ordered report prepared by a probation officer to assist the judge in determining the appropriate sentence for an adult offender

Presumptive Offence: an offence committed or alleged to have been committed by a young person age 14 but not more than 16, where there may be the disposition of an adult sentence (YCJA) sec 61 refers to the offences of: murder, manslaughter, aggravated sexual assault)

Privatization: the process of tendering contracts to private agencies to run previously public administered agencies/facilities i.e." Boot Camps"

Probation: see sec. 42 (2)(k) and sec 55 and sec 56a sentence with conditions imposed by the court that the offender serves in the community under the supervision of a probation officer, for a maximum period of up to two years

Probation/Parole Officer: a person responsible for supervising offenders on probation, parole, conditional sentence or conditional supervision

Probationer: an adult offender on probation how is supervised in the community by a probation/parole officer

Protective Custody: a specialized unit placement for an offender in custody to ensure his/her safety

Provincial Director: a person, a group or class of persons, or a body appointed or designated to perform the duties or functions of a provincial director under the Young Offenders Act

Remand Centre: jail, detention centre, where persons are detained awaiting bail, or trial such as the former Toronto Youth Assessment Centre or the Toronto Jail(Don Jail)

Reprimand: sec. 42(2) (a) of the YCJA a verbal reprimand/admonishment from the court and no other disposition is imposed

Restitution: sec. 42(2) (f) of the YCJA; a condition of probation which requires the offender to make financial compensation for injury, loss or damage to an aggrieved party

Restorative Justice: primary term related to a variety of processes which bring together people who have been affected by behaviour that has caused harm. The focus is principally on the victim, offender and others most affected by the offending behavioiur. The ultimate goal: creating ways to repair the harm that has taken place. The process may take place at pre-charge, pre-sentence, post- charge, post sentence stage of a criminal justice continuum

Restorative Justice Circle: the actual process of bring people together to explore ways of repairing harm that has taken place, originally referred to as Community and family group conferencing

Safe Schools Act: An Act to increase respect and responsibility, to set standards for safe learning and safe teaching in schools and to amend the Teaching Profession Act. Came into force 20001. Includes the discussion of the term Zero Tolerance, Code of Conduct, Expulsion Protocol, Suspension Protocol.
See: www.edu.gov.on.ca/safeschl/html.

Secure Custody: correctional facility that provides treatment, counseling, plans of care for a young persons serving custodial sentence i.e. Syl Apps Kinnark Family Centre

Sentencing Circles: a key aspect of many aboriginal communities, which encourage offenders. victims, community elders, other community members and justice officials to discuss the consequences of an event and to explore ways of addressing the event; some sentencing circles operate within the formal contemporary justice system as an alternative to the conventional sentencing process; may be part of a diversions, alternative measures component of the criminal justice system.

Social Promotion: process of promoting a child to the next grade, despite his or her inability to meet the academic requirements of the next higher grade level, in order that the person remain with his or her peers

Transformative Justice: term refers to the transformative experience of people as they participate in the circle process: a person is no longer described as a victim but rather as a whole person with many capacities and abilities to change and move forward in their life, in essence an experience of transformation from perceived weakness to realized true capacity

Wraparound Process: involves both formal and informal resources/sectors in meeting the multiple complex needs of youth. Wraparound enables the youth to participate in the development of their plan, thus giving them the impetus to change and motivation to succeed. By connecting individuals to their community and encouraging people from various services and sectors to work collaboratively, Wraparound avoids overlap and confusion.

In addition to the above, Wraparound is individual and/or family- centered, community-based, builds on strengths of the individual and/or family, and cuts across boundaries of established agencies. It is a specific process that community services and members can use to help individuals and their families who have a broad spectrum of complex needs and require collaboration of various services, as well as the involvement of family, friends and faith. One of the leaders in this process is Oolagen Community Mental Health Services. www.oolagen.org

Youth Bureau: a department within municipal police divisions which deals specifically with youth crime; not every police division has a specific youth bureau. Youth matters can be directed through the community response unit, which are part of every Ontario police division

Youth Criminal Justice Act (YCJA): replaced the Young Offenders Act (YOA) on April 1, 2003. The legislation deals with young person's age12 through 17.

Youth Justice Committees: sec 18.YCJA: Committee of citizens established by the Attorney General of Canada or designates, to assist in any aspect of the administration of the Youth Criminal Justice Act or in any programs or services for young persons

Youth Justice Court: sec.13 YCJA, court designated by the YCJA to adjudicate in all matters related to youth age 12-17

Young Offenders Act (YOA): legislation from 1984-2003 which dealt with the issues of youth in conflict with the law, replaced by the current YCJA

Young Person: a person age 12-17 and being dealt with under the YCJA, this term is to replace the term "young offender"

Youth Sentence: a sentence imposed under section 42, 51, or 59 or any sections 94 to 96 of the YCJA

Youth Worker: a person working with any designated young person designated under provincial or federal legislation

Victim Offender Mediation (VOM) and
Victim Offender Reconciliation Program(VORP):

Two of the earliest forms of restorative justice programs in Canada. Brings the offender and victim together guided by a trained mediator; may take place before, or after sentencing has transpired

Zero Tolerance: Although the Ontario government promised "zero tolerance" for bad behaviour in schools before the *Safe Schools Act* was enacted, and the *Act* prescribes "mandatory" suspensions and expulsions, the presence of mitigating factors in the current legislation precludes it from being strictly characterized as "zero tolerance". Likewise, although the TDSB Safe Schools Foundation Statement Policy speaks of "zero tolerance" and "mandatory" suspensions and expulsions, the direction to principals and teachers to apply mitigating factors in disciplinary matters precludes it from being strictly characterized as "zero tolerance". The real issue is whether there is a *practice* of "zero tolerance".

In assessing whether zero tolerance is being practiced in the school system in Ontario, it is important to keep in mind that principals and teachers are receiving two contradictory messages, one advocating "zero tolerance" and prescribing "mandatory" action and the other directing them to apply mitigating factors. Source of this definition Ontario Human Rights Commission

Suggested Web Sites

The sites referred to here will link you up to initiatives on a local, national and international level.

Restorative Justice provides many articles, links to restorative justice initiatives on an international level
http://www.restorativejustice.org

St. Leonard's Society of Canada: excellent source of links to restorative justice initiatives on a municipal, national and international level.
http://www.stleonards-london.on.ca   (Then click on Community Justice Circles in left-side menu)

Overview of Correctional Services of Canada
http://www.csc-scc.gc.ca/text/forum/restore2004/kit/16_e.shtml

Rittenhouse is a Canadian leader in the restorative, transformative justice movement.
http://www.interlog.com/~ritten/home.html

Mennonite Central Committee - initiator of many restorative justice initiatives, links with many criminal justice issues
http://www.mcc.org/canada/restorativejustice/index.html

Community Justice initiative in British Columbia, involving one on one programs with youth
http://www.gov.chilliwack.bc.ca/services/crjyda/

Triune Arts provides training videos on community healing circles and restorative justice models.
http://www.triune.ca/pages/prod/rcc4.html

Overview of Department of Justice Canada, including programs and initiatives, including aboriginal justice networks and alternative dispute resolution.
http://canada.justice.gc.ca

Overview of Solicitor General of Canada including programs and initiatives
http://www.sgc.gc.ca

Overview of the John Howard Society of Canada
http://www.johnhoward.ca/start.htm

Site of the leaders in Transformative Justice training taking place in Australia, and on an international level.
http://www.tja.com.au/

Jessica's Journey

A young lady, a beautiful girl travels to the spirit world she calls her home. Upon the back on an Eagle she rides. For it is the Eagle that flies the highest and sees the farthest of all the winged one's and is known to be the Creators Helper. Through her journey she finds the language of the heartbeat, the sound of love, peace and freedom. The very element that she has held within her from the day she was born. Jessica's journey teaches us all of the beautiful gifts the Creator has given to all of us, and how important it is to remember to honour every breath we take.

Bibliography
Restorative Justice

Suggested Readings

**These books have influenced the development
of not only this book but the
Restorative Justice workshops as well.**

Berkowitz, B. **Local Heroes,** *Lexington Press, 1985.* Inspirational stories of how people can contribute to many issues of community justice in simple and profound ways.

Braithwaite, J. **Crime, Shame and Reintegration,** *Cambridge University Press, 1989*

Brendtro, Larry; Brokenleg, Martin; Van Bockern, Steve. **Reclaiming Youth At Risk: Our Hope for the Future.***National Educational Service. 1990*

Cayley, D. **The Expanding Prison: The Crisis in Crime and Punishment and the Search for Alternatives***, Anansi Press, 1998.*

Christie, N. **Limits to Pain**, *Oxford: Blackwell, 1981.* Provides discussion on the effectiveness of informal, community intervention in addressing issues of crime.

Church Council on Justice and Corrections, **Satisfying Justice,** *1996.* Provides an incredible array of community options to help repair harm, and seek alternatives to the use of imprisonment in Canada.

Chomsky, N. **Necessayr Illusions**, *House of Anasi Press, 1989.* Provided through the CBC Massey Lecture Series, it invites us to look at social contracts in ways that affect all our social institutions.

Goleman, Daniel **Emotional Intelligence.** *. Bantam Books. 1995*

> **Working With Emotional Intelligence**. *Bantam Books. 1995*

Chelsom Gossen, Diane, **Restitution: Restructuring School Discipline** *New View Publications. 1996*

Griffiths, D. M., C. Stavrakaki & J. Summers. (2002). **Dual Diagnosis: An Introduction to the Mental Health Needs of Persons with Developmental Disabilities***. Sudbury, Ontario: Habilitative Mental Health Resource Network.*

Hart, S. &V. K. Hodson. (2003). *The Compassionate Classroom: Relationship Based Teaching and Learning*. La Crescenta, California: Centre for Non-Violent Communication.

Kohn, Alfie. (2004). *What Does It Mean to Be Well Educated?: And More Essays on Standards, Grading, and Other Follies*. Boston: Beacon Press.

____. (1999). *Punished By Rewards: The Trouble with Gold Stars, Incentive Plans, A's, Praise, and Other Bribes*. Boston: Houghton Mifflin Co.

____. (1996). *Beyond Discipline: From Compliance to Community*. Alexandria Virginia: ACSD.

Krishnamurti, J. The Awakening of Intelligence, Harper& Row, Publishers Press 1973. Provides a seminal dissertation on how to approach violence from a philosphical veiw, as well as practical processes.

Marron K., Apprenticed in Crime, 1989. Provides the best account of the youth justice system in Canada, from the perspective of not only the justice workers but the youth as well. A must read.

McKnight J. The Careless Society: Community and its Counterfits, Basic Books, 1995. Provides insightful discussion on the effectiveness of "professionalism" in addressing issues of community justice, vs seeking out the ways of community capacity building

McQuaig L. Shooting The Hippo, Viking Press, 1995. Provides discussion on the economic process of our country and the philosophy that supports the discussion... invites people to be involved in the political process.

O'Brien J., O'Brien C., and Jacob, G. Celebrating The Ordinary, Inclusion Press, 1998. Provides powerful illustration of how a people-centered approach creates a vibrant community.

Peck S. A World Wating to Be Born, Bantam Books, 1993. Provides a discourse on the effectiveness of consciously creating and supporting the practice of civility in our lives.

The Different Drum, Touchstone Books, 1987. Provides ways of developing and practicing the philosophy of community building.

Promoting Social and Emotional Learning. Association for Supervision and Curriculum Development. 1997

Ross, R. Returning to the Teachings, Penguin Books, 1996. Provides accounts of how the philosophy and practices of aboriginal justice makes a great deal of sense in our country. A beautifully written work.

Shaffer, C., Anundsen K. **Creating Community Anywhere**, *Putmanm Publishing, 1993.* Provides one of the most practical formats for building community capacity anywhere. Excellent "how to" stories.

Sharpe S., **Restorative Justice: A Vison for Healing and Change**, *Edmonton Victim Offender Mediation Society, 1998.*   An insightful and illuminating overview of the philosophy and practice of Restorative Justice in Canada.

Schumacher E.F., **Small is Beautiful: 25 years later**, *Hartley & Marks Publishers. dd* Provides the text of one of the most influential books ever written, framed with commentaries of leading figures on contemporary social thought.

Sherman, J.R. **The Magic of Humour in Caregiving**, *Pathway Books, 1995.* Provides accounts of the power of humour, as an incredible asset when dealing with issues of conflict and relationship-building.

Stevens, J. **Aikido**, *Shambala Press, 1996.* Provides the philosophy of this martial art, which has clear application to the practice of faclitating restorative justice circles.

Stuart, Judge B., **Building Community Justice Partnerships: Community Peacemaking Circles, Aboriginal Justice Learning Network, Department of Justice, Canada, 1997**

Tangney, J. Price & Dearing, R.L., **Shame and Guilt**. New York: The Guilford Press, 2002

Van Ness, D. and Heetderks Strong, K., **Restoring Justice**, *Anderson Publishing, 1997*

Weber M., **Streetkids, The Tragedy of Canada's Runaways**, *University of Toronto Press, 1991.* Provides a forum for the voices of the people so often never heard... the "kids" themselves. A must read for anyone engaged in the issues of youth and justice.

Wolin, Steven & Sybil, **The Resilient Self: How Survivors of Troubled Families Rise Above Adversity**, *Random House, 1993*

Zehr, H., **Changing Lenses: A new focus for crime and justice**, *Scottsdale Press, 1990.* Provides the most widely referenced views on restorative justice... essential to any practitioner in the field.

Bear Spirit

It is said that the Great Bear sits in the North Doorway. The direction of the medicine.

In the beginning of time our Mother the Earth had given the bear the knowledge of the medicine for with each step he takes his mighty claws dig deep into her flesh. The Bear was also given the responsibility of policing the communities for he is respected. It is above the bear this boy sits and it is above him the spirit of the Creator with his wings of life protect him. With each step in life you will be given a direction to take, look within your heart and listen to your heartbeat. The sound of the drums will lead the way.

Restorative Justice
Forms & Agreements

Conference Referral Form

Restorative Justice Agreement

Restorative Justice Conference Evaluation

Form to be Considered for Conferencing

Restorative Justice Agreement

The Restorative Justice Conference took place at _____
on _____ (date)

Participant* in the Conference (list all in attendance)

Complainant end Supporters   Accused and Supporter*   Other

_____   _____   _____

_____   _____   _____

_____   _____   _____

_____   _____   _____

_____   _____   _____

_____   _____   _____

The terms of the agreement will be supervised by: _____

Follow-up in the form of_____

_____ will take place on; _____

Terms of .Agreement   Date Fulfilled ("X" Completed)

_____   _____   ☐

_____

_____   Note: Any terms agreed to that
have not yet bun fulfilled (but
are being attempted) should be
noted as "in progress".

_____

_____   _____   ☐

_____

_____   _____   ☐

_____

(more space on back of form)

_____   _____   ☐

_____

_____

_____

_____   _____   ☐

_____

_____

_____   _____   ☐

_____

_____

_____

Conference Participant Signatures

_____   _____

_____   _____

_____   _____

_____   _____

_____   _____

_____   _____

_____   _____

Agreement Supervisor's (or facilitator's) Signature (upon completion of agreement)

_____   _____

Restorative Justice Conference Referral Form

Accused Information:

Name: _____

DOB: _____

Address:_____

_____

Referral Made By:

Name _____

Phone _____

Date _____

Phone _____

Parent/Guardian Name: _____

Phone:(w) _____ Phone:(h) _____

Address (if different from above): _____

School: Current _____ Phone _____

School: Former _____ Phone _____

School Contact _____ Phone _____ Suspension Dates:_____

Attended suspension program: Yes ☐ No ☐

Complainant Information:

Name: _____ Phone _____

School: _____ Phone _____

Parent/Guardian: _____ Phone (h) _____ (w):_____

Name: _____ Phone _____

School: _____ Phone _____

Parent/Guardian: _____ Phone (h) _____ (w):_____

Description of Incident: *Date of Incident:*

_____   _____

_____

_____

Charges Laid: Yes ☐   **No** ☐   **Please List**

_____   _____   _____

_____   _____   _____

Court Dates:

First Appearance: _____ **PreTrial:** _____ **Outcome:** _____

Restorative Justice Conference Contacts (where applicable):

Crown: _____ Phone: _____

Police Officer in Charge: _____ Phone: _____

Lawyer: _____ Phone: _____

Duty Council: _____ Phone: _____

Judge: _____ Phone: _____

Probation: _____ Phone: _____

Restorative Justice Conference: ☐ Accepted: _____

☐ Rejected: _____

Facilitator Assigned: _____

To Be Considered for a Restorative Justice Conference

Name(s) of Accused: _____   _____

_____   _____

_____   _____

Next Date of Appearance: _____

Office In Charge (OIC): _____   Division: _____

Synopsis Attached: YES ☐   NO ☐

Summary: _____

_____

_____

Undertaking: It is understood and agreed that: any admission, confession or statement accepting responsibility for a given act or omission made by a young person, relating to the incident giving rise to (he Restorative Measures Conference, shall be treated as an involuntary statement for the purposes of Young Offenders Act or Criminal Code proceedings. Specifically, the Crown Attorney's Office undertakes not to use any statement made by the participants during the Restorative Measures Conference at any later criminal proceeding.

Crown's Signature: _____   Date: _____

Waiver of Delays: It is further understood that any Intentional delay on the part of the offender in fullfilling the contract signed by all parties, including the offender, within the mandate of the Restorative Measures Conference, shall not be used as an argument for failure to be "tried in a reasonable time," as stipulated in S. 11(b) in the Charter of Rights and Freedoms. Nor shall the time between the contract entered into by all parties, including the offender, becoming null and void due to any action on the part of the offender and the resumption of Judicial proceedings, be used as an argument for failure to be "tried in a reasonable time," as stipulated in S. 11(b) of the Charter of Rights and Freedoms.

Dated at the City of |] In this _____ day of _____ 20___

Student Signature: _____   Print Name: _____

Witness/Support Person Signature: _____ Print Name: _____

Restorative Justice
Conference Evaluation

Date: _____   **Name:** _____

Role: _____   **Conf. Facilitator:** _____

How important was it for
you to be involved in a
Restorative Justice Conference?

☐   **5 - Very Important; 3 - Important; 1 - Not Important**

Comments: _____

_____

_____

_____

What did you hope to achieve through this process?

Comments: _____

_____

_____

_____

_____

Please categorize your goals for involvement in this conference:

☐   prevention   ☐   help others to learn something

☐   confront offender   ☐   openly express feelings

☐   question others about the incident ☐   gain restitution

☐   gain closure about incident   ☐   ensure clear accountability

Were your goals realilzed or fulfilled?

Comments: _____

_____

_____

_____

Were there additional benefits that you gained from participation?
Comments: _____

_____

_____

_____

To what extent do you feel
satisfied with the process?

☐   **5 - Very Satisfied; 3 - Satisfied; 1 - Not Satisfied**

Why? Please comment: _____

_____

_____

_____

_____

_____

Please check off which categories apply to the conference:

_____

_____

Please categorize your goals for involvement in this conference:

☐   expectations were clear and well explained in advance

☐   opportunity to discuss the incident and my role In the conference

☐   opportunity to process the incident at the conference

☐   the facilitator was fair

☐   I was able to express my feelings

☐   I was encouraged to be an active participant

☐   I was Involved In the decisions achieved.

Calling for Harmony

Upon the Sweatlodge a young boy reaches high with sacred pipe in hand. With his pipe in hand he calls up to the Creator to bring the Spirit of the sky's (The winged ones) and the spirit of the earth (The Bear) together. As they connect they all pray for Harmony. The winged one's ask that the rains and winds to help clean our mother earth in a good way, while the Bear ask's all the animals and plant life to do their work as well. The young boy acknowledges their prayers and with his pipe in hand he prays for the people and asks that all prayers be honoured as one, for the Calling for Harmony has begun.